"[For] anyone who wants a deeper appreciation for the full range of joys and sorrows that is the human condition."

—David Lukoff, PhD, licensed psychologist and co-president
of the Association for Transpersonal Psychology

"This book will help many, most importantly men, who struggle with similar issues to know they are not alone and that there is hope and help for them too."

—Carolyn Coker Ross, MD, MPH, author of *The Binge
Eating and Compulsive Overeating Workbook*

"Chris is an arresting storyteller. . . . This book will illuminate anyone who has had even a taste of such maladaptive behaviors and should be required reading for every therapist, counselor, minister, or instructor in the field of transpersonal psychology."

—Dorothy Walters, PhD, author of *Unmasking the
Rose: A Record of a Kundalini Initiation*

"With Chris Cole's book, the intimate link between madness and mysticism could not be more apparent. Written with precision, brutal honesty, and flare, this cautionary tale from the 'boy next door' could be the book that finally opens the mainstream to one of the great mysteries of our time."

—Sean Blackwell, author of *Am I Bipolar or Waking Up?*

"*So* raw and honest. . . . Chris leaves no stone unturned in his transformative journey."

—Debra Silverman, psychotherapist and world-renowned astrologer

"A brutally honest autobiography and case history that reveals the entanglements of addiction, bipolar illness, eating disorder, and spiritual emergence in the life of one man who has struggled for a lifetime with all four. . . . His story offers insight and hope for those who have similar afflictions and those who care for them."

—Bonnie Greenwell, PhD, author of *The Kundalini
Guide* and *The Awakening Guide*

"It takes courage, an engaging authorial voice, and a deep love for people to reveal one's winding path from significant personal struggles to heart-centered awakenings, as Chris Cole has done in *The Body of Chris.*"

—Stuart Sovatsky, PhD, author of *Advanced Spiritual
Intimacy* and *Words from the Soul*

"Chris Cole has written a daring, moving, and utterly candid account of the inner world of psychosis and bipolar disorder. I recommend it to psychiatrists and psychologists of all persuasions, and to anyone who wishes to understand the relationship between severe emotional problems and the mysteries of the human unconscious. I was transfixed by it."

—Bryan Wittine, PhD, Jungian psychoanalyst

"Chris is a perfect example of how mental illness does not discriminate—it affects the best and brightest of us all. . . . Chris is a gifted and courageous man, and his story needs to be heard. I am thankful that he is willing to share it."

—Mark E. Crawford, PhD, licensed clinical psychologist and author of *The Obsessive-Compulsive Trap*

"Chris's journey touches on many common struggles and creative solutions of our young men today. . . . Chris's story offers young men more choices, greater freedom for self-expression and deeper communication, and increased emotional intelligence."

—Francis Kaklauskas, PsyD, Graduate School of Psychology at Naropa University

"As a mental health psychotherapist specializing in eating disorders, addiction, and chronic mental illness, I believe that Chris's story is not only his truth, [but also] a journey that all of us can relate with. . . . This work is a game changer."

—Joseph R. Eiben, eating psychology counselor and holistic nutritionist

"In *The Body of Chris*, Chris Cole opens the window to his soul and allows us to observe a remarkable journey through childhood insecurities, alcohol and drug dependency, eating disorders, and bipolar psychosis. . . . Anyone interested in what it means to be a human being can learn a great deal from this book."

—Michael Washburn, PhD, author of *The Ego and the Dynamic Ground: A Transpersonal Theory of Human Development*

THE
BODY OF CHRIS

THE
BODY OF CHRIS

A Memoir of Obsession, Addiction, and Madness

CHRIS COLE

INKSHARES

Published by Inkshares Inc., San Francisco, California
www.inkshares.com

Edited and designed by Girl Friday Productions
www.girlfridayproductions.com

Cover design by John Barnett
Photography by Andrew Thomas Lee © 2014

ISBN: 9781941758144
Library of Congress Control Number: 2015938848

First edition

Printed in the United States of America

For Tay-Tay Magpie.

Table of Contents

PART ONE: GENESIS

Part Two: Exodus

Part Three: Revelation

Epilogue: Go in Love

"Out beyond ideas
of wrongdoing and rightdoing,
there is a field.
I'll meet you there."

—Rumi

Part One

GENESIS

Chapter 1

ORIGINAL SIN

As a child, I thought my parents were perfect. I wondered if they were really my parents, if maybe there had been a switch at the hospital or some immaculate intervention they would disclose to me once I was older. I sometimes imagined them dying—in a car crash, on an airplane, murdered by evil villains—and I would feel a strange mix of profound relief and sadness right before asking God for forgiveness. Their love was overwhelming, and I was afraid that I wouldn't be able to be what they wanted me to be, even though they always insisted: "We just want you to be happy."

Dad's high-school letter jacket lived in the coat closet, and when I put it on, it felt heavy, like the large lead aprons in hospital X-ray rooms. On the letters were frayed icons of glory, a football and basketball stitched into the fabric. Dad tried to teach me basketball, but I couldn't make strong swishing sounds and shout "Nothing but net!" the way he always did. I wanted to be just like him, so he encouraged me to keep practicing. Maybe one day, I could win at this game of life too.

Mom had been a cheerleader in high school and college. I would watch in amusement as she taught my little sister, Allison, her cheers, privately wishing I could play along. Only girls were cheerleaders, though. Whenever I was sad, Mom cheered me up. She told me how great I was, how the other kids were scared and insecure, and that was why they hurt me at school. I would do extraordinary things. I could be whatever I wanted to be, whoever I wanted to be. I tried to believe her. She was the most precious gift in my life. I hoped to find a wife just like her, the way Dad had.

I liked it when they told me stories about their lives before I existed—how they'd fallen in love when they were twelve, how Mom used to go to church with Dad's family, how Dad had saved up all his money one summer, scooping ice cream at Baskin-Robbins, so he could buy her a ring. He proposed in the church parking lot in their modest Louisiana hometown. They were still just kids, and Mom told me she couldn't legally drink at her own wedding. Dad showed me how strong his forearms were, crediting that summer at Baskin-Robbins from a decade before. They would kiss each other while telling me stories and laugh when I'd cop a grin and exclaim, "Gross!" But later, alone in my room, I would think it was the most beautiful thing I'd ever seen and wonder where my future wife was right at that moment and if maybe she was thinking of me too.

School made me cry a lot. My parents would try to comfort me, but I was inconsolable. "You learn to deal with it," Dad assured me with teary eyes, referring to our sensitive temperaments, an affliction that had befallen the males of our family for at least three generations. Poppy, my paternal grandfather, cried every time he spoke from the heart. Poppy's father gambled and drank, so maybe he was sensitive too, and nobody knew it.

"It's just in the genes," Mom cheerfully insisted, but her favorite mantra confused me.

I wiped my eyes and looked up at her. "Why did God give me bad genes?"

She hesitated. "Nobody knows," she said. "You'll have to ask Him when you get to heaven."

I had a lot of questions for the big guy upstairs, like, *Why can Mom eat apple pie à la mode for dinner and not get fat?* and *How come Dad has so much self-discipline, but I can't stop sneaking snacks?*

My genes sucked. I was *husky*. I knew this because when we'd go to the mall to buy new clothes, Mom always asked the employees, "Where is your husky section?" I didn't fit into regular pants, and Mom had to take me to the tailor to get my jeans hemmed. When my second-grade class nominated me to represent us in a fashion-show fund-raising event for the school, I was unable to fit into any of the clothes, so Mom had to buy me grown-man pants. After the alterations, it looked like I was wearing a parachute down the runway.

I was only a little kid, but I understood that my body was kind of a lemon. In addition to being husky, I was asthmatic. The doctors said that if I lost some weight, it might go away, but according to my parents, the asthma was in the genes too. Dad still had to use his inhaler sometimes. Plus he had sleep apnea and snored really loud, so he had to wear a machine mask at night that made him look as if he should be flying a fighter jet or rocketing into space. Mom had fibromyalgia, which made her need lots of naps and caused her body to hurt for no reason. She feared she might be in a wheelchair soon. She told me, "We are lucky to have modern medicine; otherwise, we might not be alive." I didn't feel gratitude though; I believed there had been an error, that God had made a mistake, that my body was an accident.

What went on *down there* was particularly problematic. As much as I wanted to, and no matter how hard I tried, I couldn't control my bladder during sleep. As young as I was, all I really knew was that peeing the bed wasn't normal. I remember the crinkling of plastic underneath my sheets, my parents helping me get changed out of urine-soaked pajamas in the middle of the night, and the fear and embarrassment I felt whenever sleeping over at a friend's house.

I had a recurring dream in which I'd be shuffling down the long, dark, carpeted hallway of our quaint Atlanta home. I'd turn right into the bathroom, lift up the toilet seat, apprehensively point my member downward, and finally decide to start peeing, only I was really just urinating all over myself again, and I'd wake up frustrated and confused as to why my mind kept playing tricks on me. My parents told me, "It's not your fault," but I was angry that I couldn't control my body in ways others could.

I was born into a medical family, which helped me understand my health concerns but also kept me pretty neurotic about germs and genetics and diseases. My mom was a neonatal nurse practitioner, which basically meant that she cared for sick or premature babies in the intensive care unit. My father was in his third year of medical school when I was born, and he eventually became an oculoplastic surgeon, a physician who specialized in ophthalmology (eyes) and plastic surgery. I always wanted to be a doctor, just like Dad.

When Allison was born, my mom bought me a doll to play with, in order to teach me about babies. Naturally, at two years old, I enjoyed mimicking my parents' care for my baby sister. But my mom recalls how disturbed her father was at the idea of me having a doll. As he saw it, "Dolls are for girls." The gender lines were drawn quickly. I was encouraged to be a good big brother and protect my sister from harm, a role I relished. I would walk down the street with my plastic sword in hand, ready to defend against anyone who might do wrong by her.

By the time my brother, Tyler, was born two years later, I had taken on the role of mommy's little helper. I was encouraged to support my mom by holding Allison's hand in the parking lot, trading my whole cookie for Tyler's broken one, and basically being patient and compliant while my mom did her best to deal with three children in diapers. I remember thinking of Tyler and Allison as children, and of myself as something separate, less than an adult but certainly not a child. I permitted my siblings a freedom that I didn't allow myself—to be less than perfect, to mess up, and to struggle. I was superior, more responsible, burdened in ways I couldn't nail down.

I was always the fat kid, though I was slow to understand what this particular label entailed. I became aware of food rules and knew that there were treats I wasn't supposed to eat except on special occasions. There was the time I joined the Cub Scouts and wore my orange tiger shirt to school for the inaugural meeting. All day, I looked forward to congregating with my buddies over cookies and other snacks. My parents somehow either forgot to sign the permission slip or forgot to pay, so I wasn't allowed in the room. I was so sad that I couldn't have any cookies. I sulked in the fluorescent-lit hallway, trying to hold back the tears, then dragged my feet along what seemed like a mile stretch back to the car-pool lot. My forbidden fruit had been identified, and the more it was forbidden, the more I felt deprived.

My body often invited unwanted attention. I was terrified of the car-pool teacher. When we'd pull up for school, she would get all excited and pinch my cheeks. It hurt badly, and I wondered how my face didn't bruise. I would walk around the entire building and enter a side door just to avoid her. I hated having pudgy cheeks. I didn't like that people were constantly commenting on my body. Boys called me "fat." Girls called me "cute." Adults found me "adorable," and I was fast to learn that this was all a commentary on my body shape.

Physical-education classes and after-school sports were a nightmare. It was hard to run because I would wheeze. I was allergic to pollen, grass, ragweed, dust, and really just about every environmental allergen under the sun. Play became synonymous with exercise, and I really didn't like to exercise. Even recess was tricky. The boys would separate from the girls and play a sport on the field. Girls would play on the playground. If I played with the boys, I almost always got picked last. In the event of an anomaly, I knew it was due to one of the captains taking pity on me. I liked playing with the girls. I'd get them to chase me around the playground and spank me. I identified girls as the safer sex.

Since my dad was finishing medical school, we moved a good bit as he transitioned from poor student to wealthy surgeon. I was born in New Orleans, but I don't remember anything from the time we lived there. Then there was Nashville, where we lived in a small ranch-style brick house on a plot of land that was probably under an acre, but I felt as if our home were on a farm. Dad used to drive over the front yard when he left for work, pretending to lose control of the wheel, threatening to crash into the large front window of the house, where Mom and I watched with bated breath and laughed hysterically. By the time I turned seven, we were in our second home, this time in Atlanta, the same kind of house, just in a bigger city—and we weren't finished yet, since one day we'd move to a mansion with a pool in the backyard, but not until I was in the fourth grade. In 1992, money was still tight, and Mom worked overnight shifts at the hospital to bring home the bacon.

Each time we moved houses, I switched schools, and each time I switched, the anxiety would get worse. Because I was the fat kid, it took more time to get to know my classmates and win them over. I had to rely on my personality. Each new school brought with it a new set of first impressions, a new set of bullies, and a new set of rules I had to learn how to follow. The rules were really piling up. There were classroom rules, dress-code rules, gender rules, food rules, exercise rules, play rules, rules about health, rules about manners, rules about behavior toward adults, rules about everything. I was becoming an expert in the distinctions between right and wrong, good and evil. The rules kept me safe, but at the same time imprisoned me.

When I was nervous or embarrassed, I blushed, and then I would get redder the more I tried to stop. Kids would point out, "Chris is getting red," and I would flush with terror. At the same time that I wanted to hide, I was starving for attention. I needed to be seen and heard, and I found out how to use being fat to my advantage. If I made fun of myself, everyone laughed. It also lessened the power of cruel little boys who might hope to hurt me. I would lift up my shirt and use ventriloquism, folding my belly into a mouth and demanding of my friends, "Feed tummy more cookie!"

Despite my social anxiety, I became a popular kid who genuinely enjoyed joking around and goofing off. The problem was that I developed a division that cut right through me. There was the Chris everyone saw, and there was the secret Chris who felt a great deal of pain. I knew that big boys were tough, and when it came to creating that image, I was a budding perfectionist. But on the inside, I was just a really sensitive little boy, and the disconnect that began as a crack would eventually widen into a canyon, one large enough to swallow me whole.

Chapter 2

SHAPEDOWN

Everybody has a body, but my body was different. The pediatrician identified my weight as a health concern by showing me a growth chart. One side of the graph measured height, and the other side measured weight. A middle line defined the exact measurement of normal, and the farther I deviated, the more problematic my doctor found me to be. I was assigned a little dot. "This is where you are," he said, pointing high above the desired range. I was stranded out there, a lone dot, lost in the abyss of light gray graphing paper.

I ate so I could grow up to be big and strong like Dad, but my body wasn't exactly cooperating. I needed to change.

"You must eat healthier and exercise," the doctor explained.

If I weren't already harboring suspicions about my inadequacy, now I was being objectively told by a medical professional that my body was not okay. That I was not okay.

Mom was there with me, and she looked down. "That's not so bad, right, Chris? We can do that."

But I didn't want to change, and I didn't think I could either.

I was in first grade, and we still lived in Nashville at the time. My parents were given instructions to enroll me in a program at the children's hospital called Shapedown. The classes were an initiative to combat childhood obesity. A war was about to be waged between the doctors and me, but I'd already begun preparing for battle, refusing all of my parents' prior efforts to teach me healthier eating habits.

My mom remembers me having a distorted body image, which might have been denial but could have just been my inability to comprehend weight concerns at such a young age. The hospital administrators gave all of the kids a piece of paper with different body shapes drawn side by side, and told us to circle the shape that best reflected our own body. I chose the skinny one. It was a test, so I picked the right answer.

I scanned the room to size up my competition. All the other kids looked like miniature versions of their parents, and most of them seemed to have a difficult time moving around. My dad was above average height, with a burly build exaggerated slightly by his full beard; my friends said he looked like a lumberjack. He told me that he had struggled with his weight his whole life and that he could be three hundred pounds if he let himself go, but he believed that "nothing tastes better than thin feels." Mom was a petite blond beauty; one day soon, my buddies would call her a MILF. She had a wicked sweet tooth, but she skipped meals to compensate. So I showed no obvious signs of having inherited a familial problem. Some of the other kids had their whole family there, but Allison and Tyler were skinny, so they didn't have to go. I was the lone sufferer in my family, except for Poppy, who looked like Santa Claus and said he had been "fat and happy" his whole life.

I'm just fat; these kids are obese, I assured myself, refusing to acknowledge any concern about my body. Already armed with a few subtle defenses, I braved the black-and-white depictions of my gray-scaled void. Fruits and vegetables didn't feel like easy solutions for this hungry soul.

Shapedown was like a special school for fat kids. They wanted us to experience the joy of exercise, so they had us jam out to eighties rock and follow along with an aerobics video featuring a bunch of ladies wearing huge white high-tops and scrunchy neon socks. The plastic stair-stepping platforms they made us use were the bane of my existence. *How much longer?* I wondered, anxiously awaiting permission to cease fire.

We had nutrition classes, where we learned that all our favorite foods were bad. We talked a lot about our families' dietary habits, but all I could understand was that I was fat, lacked discipline, and liked food more than the rest of my family.

During classes, the hospital staff fed us apples, while they peppered us with more food rules. There were bad foods: sweets, junk food, fried food, fat, and sugar; and there were good foods: grains, vegetables, and fruits. There was a big, colorful food triangle that looked to me like the eighth wonder of the world; it showed which foods we should eat the most of and which foods we should avoid. I was a good student, so I got it: I'd been a very bad boy.

A silent rebellion commenced with ardent devotion, the beginning of a coup they'd never discover. I distanced myself psychologically from so-called healthy behavior. I didn't need it. I didn't want it. I started sneaking food whenever I could. No matter how much I was given to eat, I felt deprived. Mom and Dad were on the same team as the doctors, and so they became my enemies. Their food was "healthy," something that was "good," and here I was, desperately desiring to be bad.

Despite my ill feelings about health, my parents and pediatrician held fast to the instructions issued by Shapedown. Low-fat and fat-free thinking dominated the dieting philosophy of the eighties and nineties, the idea being that if you didn't eat fat, you wouldn't get fat. I just might have honestly been hungry. My lunches were loaded with fruit, pretzels, carrot sticks, fat-free ranch dressing, low-fat yogurt, low-fat string cheese, and sandwiches with lean meats and mustard. Eating became a chore that was occasionally rewarded with a treat, provided I could compensate with adequate exercise.

During school lunch period, I would do my best to trade away items and basically beg for food from other kids. It always amazed me how much food would go uneaten, food that I was dying to have. I would nab entire candy bars, peanut-butter crackers, fruit snacks, and leftover sandwiches with *real* mayonnaise. It shocked me that other kids wanted the healthy food I had. My buddy Henry would trade his chocolate bar for my pretzels. "What a sucker," I'd gleefully snicker to myself.

Withholding the truth became a necessary part of existence. I became an expert liar. If I held eye contact and disclosed some intimate detail of my cognitive process, they'd have no choice but to believe me. My eating behavior away from my parents was a secret between my classmates and me. My friends would throw their leftovers in the middle of the table; first come, first served. I'd never moved faster in my life. Mom would call my teachers and talk to other parents. My friends would tell me, "Sorry, my mom says I'm not allowed to trade with you anymore."

My suffering was subconscious; the pain was too tough to touch, an elusive hurt just beyond my grasp. I couldn't articulate or understand the source of my shame, and the more conscious I became of food and weight concerns, the less willing I was to discuss any discomfort with my parents. I remember going to the drive-thru with my family, where Tyler and Allison would each get a Happy Meal. Even though my mom cautiously encouraged me to get something else, it felt like she was damning me. I was the one who needed to eat healthfully. I got the unhappy meal, and then I would wish for the French fries I didn't have long after the meal was over.

As the years went on, my family did the best they could to maneuver around my eating woes. We bought all sorts of altered foods that might spare me a few calories and lessen the feelings of deprivation. There were brands that sold modified versions of junk food. I would binge on entire sleeves of fat-free devil's food cookies, a sinless indulgence, or so I thought. I'd take a spoon to a half gallon of reduced-fat ice cream, my guilt-free, high-sugar, low-fat treat. Words like *nutrition* and *health* became code words, meaning "food for fat kids." *I can have as many as I want; they're healthy*, I'd convince myself, standing in the open pantry, privately partaking in my favorite pastime.

None of it made sense. I just loved to eat. I knew I was fat; that was made abundantly clear, but the trait didn't define me at first. I was fat, my buddy Bryant was black, my other pal Tim was short—these were just observations people made; there weren't character implications attached to them yet. Unfortunately, I had plenty of time to catch up, and before long, I was constantly aware of my size and obsessed with what I was eating or *not* eating. Despite my parents' and medical professionals' earnest efforts to help me live a healthier life, I was gaining more and more weight.

Chapter 3

GOOD SPORT

I wasn't athletic, so I had to be a good sport. My body wasn't doing me any favors. I was fat, slow, and asthmatic. I didn't like to run, and sometimes I couldn't run, and most often I couldn't tell the difference. In no particular order, I'd find myself in an anxious panic, trying to catch up, struggling to breathe, and deciding how long to suffer before quitting. Maybe it happened all at once. I appreciated positive messages regarding adversity, sound bites like, "What doesn't kill you only makes you stronger." I figured I'd be pretty strong one day. I didn't want to die; I don't think anyone really does, but I frequently wanted another water break.

Every once in a while, I wouldn't stop. I'd be running sprints, gasping for air, too embarrassed to call a time-out so I could shuffle to the sidelines for my inhaler. A few public puffs on my medicinal aerosol canister were humiliating enough to make me want to die of hypoxia instead. My mom would come pick me up from practice to find me purple-lipped, whistling soft words at her, seemingly oblivious to the situation's severity. She'd rush me to the emergency room so I could hit the hospital's enormous vaporizer machine for about an hour. My face felt tingly as the albuterol kicked in. I would be mortified upon my return to practice because Mom reamed all of my coaches, educating them on the signs of an asthma attack and berating them for yelling at me, "Pick it up, Cole!"

Every season of my childhood was marked by whatever sport I was playing at the time. I loved sports. I didn't love them in the conventional sense, but I loved them nonetheless. Sports were my entire social life, so I made it work. You didn't have to be athletic to be good at sports. Rewards were everywhere. I got a trophy for being the best sport on my basketball team. I wondered if the worst kid on the team always won the award for sportsmanship, but regardless, I was happy to get recognized for my positive attitude. I got another trophy for being most improved on my middle-school baseball team, the year after getting cut for not being able to hit second base from the outfield. Even in defeat, there were wins to be had. My attitude, my effort, and my conduct were all opportunities for success. I would not be denied.

Sports taught me how to think, and, influenced by Dad's daily dosage of self-help inspiration and Mom's optimistic outlook, I began to view competition as a matter of perspective. Talent was the most obvious measurable category, but there were many ways to play the game. If you lost gracefully, you were a good sport; otherwise, you were a sore loser. I learned quickly that how I lost, and how I approached my lack of talent, was a game I needed to get good at. People didn't care all that much about whether or not I was good at the game, but they cared a whole lot about how I related to my shortcomings. At least in front of my coaches and peers, I stopped acknowledging my difficulty, compensating with optimism and positivity. Reality was up for debate; it was all relative.

Everything I needed to know I learned in sports. There were always two teams. There were the good guys and the bad guys, and which ones were good and which ones were bad depended on which team we were on. There were the others, over there, and they sucked. We didn't say that, though. We said stuff like "good luck," and "may the best man win," and "it's not whether you win or lose but how you play the game." Really, we knew we were better—because red was a more dominant color than blue, lions were tougher than bears, and we secretly understood that God loved us more.

My family moved for the last time when I was in the fourth grade, landing me in Sandy Springs, an affluent city adjacent to Atlanta. We joined Riverside, the neighborhood swim and tennis club. All my best friends were my teammates at one point or another, and we would stay good friends well into adulthood.

There was Bobby, who always plugged his nose when he jumped in the water and was kind of sensitive, like me. He would cry in front of everybody, though; I held the waterworks until I got home.

There was Joe, whose dad made him drink weight gainer because he was so skinny. I would jealously watch him choke down these huge, delicious-looking vanilla milkshakes like he was taking medicine. Joe's mom called his dad "Big Daddy," but I thought my dad was bigger than him.

There was Luke, who was really nice to me, and who went to a special primary school for his dyslexia but never talked about it. His house was the best sleepover spot because he had a huge basement and his parents rarely came downstairs.

There was Henry and his best friend, Jason. Both were athletic phenoms, and we would all debate which one was better at sports. Jason threw the hardest at butts-up, but Henry was faster, and they both played on a highly competitive traveling baseball team.

Then there was Alex, who was a total goofball. I liked him best, partly because he was a little chubby too. He wouldn't spend the night out because he'd watched the horror film *It* with his buddy Sam, and the clown had scared the shit out of him. When we had sleepovers, his folks would pick him up right before the rest of us went to bed, at least until we were in middle school.

We all crushed on older girls at the club; I remember only one girl my age. Her name was Jesse, and she was also my next-door neighbor.

Eventually, I went to middle school with the whole Riverside crew, and some of us even went to college together.

When it came time for our actual swim meets against rival clubs, I would hide in the bathroom and pretend to be pooping so I wouldn't have to race. The coaches didn't really bother me too much about it, because every time I did compete, all the other children would be out of the water drying off by the time I finally touched the wall, so it wasn't like I was costing our team any points. Other than losing all my races, the main reason I skipped was that I wasn't crazy about taking my shirt off and bending over on the big metal starting blocks for all my friends to witness. I was grateful my parents didn't make me wear one of those Speedos like Jesse's little brother had to wear.

Over time, my mind became my most valuable asset, and my personality was my gift. My body was my problem, the thing that got in the way. I heard people say, "Play to your strengths," so I did. I was more like a mascot than a player, cheering on my teammates, making my friends laugh, and offering positive antidotes to any negativity in the dugout. I was a good teammate, and I received fair praise for my efforts. Sports taught me that there were endless games within the game, and that I could still be a winner. It was easier to be good at a different game than to be better at the one everyone else was playing.

The division between my mind and my body grew greater. I felt very good about my positive approach to being bad. My strengths were solidified. My humor, kindness, and positivity were great assets to any team. Still, I had this body that didn't work right. I wanted a better body, and everyone—my parents, doctors, coaches—all told me it was possible. If I could just eat healthier and exercise more, then I would have it all. I convinced myself that my body was my only problem, that if I were skinny, then I would be perfect.

When I wanted to, it was easy to change my mind. I could do it very quickly; I just needed a different vantage point, new information, and a reason to alter reality. My body wasn't so kind. I had to work hard and long to change my body, and the whole thing was exhausting. I wished I didn't have to eat. I imagined how amazing it would be just to take a pill and be done with it. Dad would coach me, "Remember, Chris, mind over matter." Clearly, there was something the matter with my mind, because no matter how hard I tried to lose weight, it didn't matter. Every time I attempted to eat less, I would just get hungry and binge.

Oddly enough, eating badly was a reward for playing sports. Treats and junk food always accompanied sport activities. After every baseball game, we got coupons redeemable at the concession stand. At all swim meets there was a ton of candy and baked sweets for sale. No matter if we won or lost, we almost always went out for pizza or Mexican food after the game. I could have as much chips and salsa as I wanted. I prayed my mom and dad wouldn't come to the restaurant with me so no one would judge how much I was eating. God still judged me, so I prayed a lot.

I spent a great deal of my childhood praying for rain. Some of my fondest memories took place in the dugout of my baseball games. We weren't actually playing baseball—just sitting together, telling yo' mama jokes, blowing bubbles with our gigantic wads of bright green watermelon Big League Chew, seeing who could spit a sunflower seed shell the farthest onto the slick field. The drumming of heavy summer showers against the flat concrete slab above my head was something spiritual, a peace offering from God assuring me of safety. I feigned disappointment while my teammates complained about the game's delay, silently basking in our fleeting camaraderie as pine-riding equals. I'd ask Heavenly Father just to finish the job and call the game off, so we could all go out for pizza. Sometimes, He obliged. Maybe it was because I wore my socks really high that game.

Chapter 4

BLACK AND WHITE

God had picked me for the white team, but I wondered if He'd made a mistake. My body seemed entirely unworthy of my soul.

Mom had been raised in the Church of Latter-Day Saints, and she said the Mormons used to believe God was punishing black people, cursing them with dark skin. But the black kids were always nicer to me. There must be something about oppression that makes people kind. Every bully I ever met was a white boy; they were the ones always causing me trouble. Whenever I went to a new school, I sought out the black kids; they were much more friendly. It was plain to see: the blacks had a monopoly on soul.

I came to understand the importance of body size around the same time I realized the significance of both genitalia and melanin. The differences between having a penis or a vagina were explained much more clearly than the differences between having dark or light skin tones. I had a penis, so I was supposed to like sports and violence and colors other than pink. The rules about being white were not as easily ascertained. I realized the most important rule of being white though: pretend skin color doesn't exist. It made all the other rules about race impossible to follow.

The best part about life, as far as I could tell, was breaking the rules. I liked food I wasn't supposed to eat. I'd play house with the girls during recess. I'd even daydream about one day falling in love and getting married and having a family, the sort of thing only girls were supposed to do. Whenever I had to behave, that was when I most enjoyed acting out. The rules of blacks and whites were fun ones to break, especially since everyone acted like they didn't exist.

My parents gave me an old-timey radio to play with, and I naturally gravitated toward V-103, the local Atlanta R & B station. I would listen to it for hours, turning the dial back and forth between that and country music. One night, when it was time to say my prayers before bed, I broke out into a rap: "Yo, dear God, thank you for my mother, my father, my sister, and my brother!" It had my folks in stitches.

The black kids at school seemed to be laughing with me more than at me. I liked black culture, and the fact that my love for the black arts made my buddies laugh was all the more inspiring. Their favorite bit was when I'd dance and sing to the 1994 cult classic "Tootsee Roll" by 69 Boyz. One of them announced to the others, "I didn't know white boys could dance like that!" I didn't understand what being white had to do with dancing, but I was excited to go home that day and practice my moves in the mirror. To borrow MC Hammer's line, I was "too legit to quit."

My peers started dropping more and more hints about the differences between whites and blacks. I found out I was a "cracker" in the fourth grade, sitting at the black table in the cafeteria. Alicia asked me, "Chris, how many crackers in the box?" I was confused. "What box?" I asked, trying to understand the question. "Just pick a number," she insisted. "Um, okay, three?" The moment I started to say *three*, she snapped her fingers in my face, sharply cocked her head to the side, and asserted, "You one of 'em." I didn't get it.

One of the saddest days of my childhood was when my mom explained to me that Jamal's mother wouldn't allow him to come to my birthday party because I was "a rich white kid." I don't know how Jamal's mom came to this conclusion, or why my mom thought I should know, but for the first time in my life, an adult had told me confidently that racism was alive and well. Prior to this, I had only ever heard of racism in history class, as if it were long gone, like Egyptians and the dinosaurs.

I bounced between various public schools as we moved up the socioeconomic ladder during my dad's medical training, and in middle school, after applying for two years, I finally arrived at the mecca: I was accepted to Holy Innocents' Episcopal School, the neighborhood private school where all my best friends went. A less-diverse universe was thrust upon me, and I never looked back. I remember only a few things about the transition: there were hardly any black kids, we all had to wear uniforms, and most of all, I was ecstatic to finally go to school with my Riverside buddies, since I had previously been the only one of us in public school.

It didn't take me long to adjust. Life was easier once everyone was white, wealthy, and Christian. I started trusting my tribe more. Within a year, mixed-race friendships were a thing of the past. I realized there were way more white kids appropriating black culture in private school than in public school, so I had finally found my people.

I spent my early adolescent years listening to gangster rap. Intuitively, I got it: it's hard being a gangster. For Halloween, we all dressed up in colorful camouflage outfits and called ourselves the "No Limit Soldiers." We donned fake jewelry from mall kiosks, crossed our arms, sagged our pants, and threw up arbitrary gang signs at the doorsteps of our conservative suburban neighbors. Nobody thought much of it, or at least they followed rule number one and didn't say anything.

I didn't think my parents were racists, and I was even told Poppy had championed some early segregation reform in his heyday, but the idea that I might have descended from slave owners still repulsed me. Every Atlanta school I attended would take field trips to the King Center downtown. Martin Luther King Jr. seemed to me to be the closest thing I'd ever witnessed to Jesus. Then I heard Jesus wasn't actually white the way the pictures depicted, and that confirmed everything I needed to know. I longed to be more colorful. The blacks had something to care deeply about, a cause of incredible significance. I cried every time I heard Dr. King's famous "I Have a Dream" speech. I tried not to let anyone see how moved I was. Boys weren't supposed to cry. The pain of the world was too much to bear, but I had to stay strong.

The idea that God had granted me such an undeserved advantage over my darker brethren left me utterly bemused. The biggest problem? God had made me this way. The guilt of being rich and white was insurmountable and gave me constant reason to contemplate God's divine plan. It took a great deal of creativity to even begin rationalizing this dissonance, since God was the ultimate cause for every effect. My conclusion? God had chosen me for greatness and was thus granting me extraordinary opportunity. I had better not waste it. If I didn't approach perfection, I'd be letting God down. There was no greater sin than squandering God's gifts.

I chose the egomaniacal route because the alternative, that an all-powerful God could let people suffer in such a way, or allow people to cause such suffering, was incredibly cruel. In my family's worldview, where God called all the shots, suffering was deserved and prosperity was entrusted. I heard enough messages of blacks' inferiority, that they were overplaying the "race card," constantly looking for handouts, and refusing to forgive long-forgotten transgressions. Over time, I learned that many blacks were uneducated, lazy, and angry, though these messages weren't explicitly taught. Words like *poor* and *crime* became synonymous with *black*, as implied in the media, in music, in my own observations about Atlanta's homeless population. I knew this was wrong, so I decided I was that much more worthy of my good fortune. My privilege and perfection-ism went hand in hand.

I regarded black culture with a near mystical reverence. Whites just had food; blacks had *soul food*. We had white supremacy; they had *black power*. I grew haunted by the suspicion that I was on the wrong team, or that perhaps this was why God had sent me to earth in the first place—so I could be an agent for change, for peace, for equality. Despite stories of slavery, I associated being black with freedom. They seemed free to feel more emotion, to act out, to wear flashy clothes and jewelry. My affinity was so strong that I wondered if I had been black in a past life.

The more I learned about slavery, segregation, and the civil rights movement, the more sure I became that I myself had no grounds for suffering. I felt so close to Dr. King's dream. I wanted to be on the team for justice. I wanted to tell the world about my dreams too. I wanted to shout God's glory from the mountaintops, but I was wealthy and white, so I had no legitimate fight. My battle was an invisible one, a struggle between me and God. I knew I had a long way to go to be worthy of His grace.

Chapter 5

KARATE KID

I might have been resilient, but I didn't have much fight. To toughen me up, my parents thought it would be a good idea to enroll me in karate classes.

I stood still across from another little boy at the beginning of my first sparring match. Our parents encouraged us from the stands: "Hit him! Go on! Hit him!" and so, reluctantly, I did. The boy began to cry, and then I turned to my parents in terror and began crying myself. I begged my parents not to make me go back. I didn't want to hurt anybody. Jesus had instructed us to "turn the other cheek," so I was incredibly confused as to why all these adults needed me to fight. After I complained enough, my parents let me off the hook. I was a lover, not a fighter.

I knew I was strong. Whenever my friends would arm wrestle, I always won. I had a lot of practice with my dad, even though he always beat me. *I may be fat, but I'm also strong,* I'd recite to myself, affirming my masculinity. Other boys in my class would lose to girls in arm-wrestling matches, and I couldn't understand how that was possible. The older we got, the more we found ways to decide who was stronger and, eventually, who would win in a fight.

As boys, we were always flirting with physical confrontation. I didn't like any of it, not even officially sanctioned forms like football or wrestling. One time I sprained my ankle when Henry tackled me, and I just ended up angry whenever we horsed around. I hated any and all fighting; it made me uncomfortable, and there was nothing fun about it. In middle school, guys would give each other "dead arms" by trading punches. No thanks. Alex was constantly initiating the flinch game, where if you made someone flinch, you got one free punch. There were titty twisters, wet willies, and all sorts of other games boys played to break physical boundaries with each other. We'd even slap each other in the testicles and punch our thumbs up one another's butts in the hallways. I rarely found it amusing.

One of my middle-school friends, James, got in his head one day the burning question: "Hey, Chris, which one of us do you think would win in a fight?"

"I don't know," I sheepishly replied. "I don't want to fight you, dude."

Looking back, I can see why he was attracted to me as a worthy opponent. We were stark opposites as far as our bodies were concerned. He was tall and skinny, and I was short and fat. I thought we were buddies, but that rarely had anything to do with these matters. I used to sleep over at his house. As far as I could tell, he liked me.

James started making a lot of comments about my body one week at school. This was fairly common, so I didn't think much of it until it persisted over days. He announced, "Chris doesn't look that fat from the front, but from the back, he doubles in size," which was a particularly cutting observation, because I would slouch my shoulders forward to try to keep my man boobs from protruding. It was the sort of intelligent, calculated insult that confirmed my deepest fears, that my peers were closely studying me, and my every move was under scrutiny.

James started upping the ante, making comments about how he could kick my ass. He'd constantly bring up this imaginary fight between the two of us. Normally, this scenario was purely hypothetical, not to be considered a direct challenge, but he was laying it on pretty thick. I was getting very uncomfortable around him, and I couldn't understand where this was all coming from. The threat set off an intuitive, primal fear. *Could it be that this lanky kid is picking a fight with me purely over my body shape?*

I had never been in a fight, and there had been plenty of prior occasions when I'd been verbally harassed, but no physical activity had occurred, so I tried to ignore my concerns. Then, a few days later, one morning before school, James and I were hanging out, walking the hallway and waiting for class, when he again started suggesting we fight.

"What the hell? I don't want to fight you!" I tried to explain, but it didn't matter; he was committed. James rolled up some school papers and began hitting me with them. I pushed him away from me, and he grabbed the receiver from a nearby pay phone and hit me over the head with it. He then threw his first punch, striking me in the face. I was officially in a fight.

What happened next was that I lost control of myself for the first time I can remember. I wrestled him down into a headlock and began punching him repeatedly in the head while shouting, "What the fuck is your problem?"

Eventually, I released him, and we went our separate ways. I was hysterical. My body was shaking, and I began to weep, retreating to a nearby bathroom. My mouth had gotten cut on my braces, but otherwise, I was unharmed. Physically I was not in any pain, but emotionally and mentally I was hurting. I stared myself down in the mirror, most concerned with hiding evidence of my tears. I felt incredibly unsafe. I was afraid he'd retaliate, and we'd have to fight again.

It didn't take long for the story to circulate around school: "Chris beat up James." We were both called in to the principal's office and told to stay away from each other. This was weird, because it wasn't a very large class and we were friends with the same boys. I kept asking my buddies, "Why did he try to fight me?" There was an unspoken understanding that boys just fought sometimes, but I wanted an explanation. I felt bad for fighting, both because I knew I wasn't supposed to and because I didn't want to hurt anyone. I vacillated between feeling bad for James and mad at him. I was also scared of myself; something had snapped in me.

James was the richest kid I knew. I had been on his baseball team, and he hosted practice at his house because his family had built an entire baseball field on their gated estate. Their megamansion had multiple wings and an intercom system so they could all talk to each other. I wondered if he needed to prove himself somehow, if maybe he was compensating and I was merely the unlucky recipient of his pain. "Boys will be boys" just didn't suffice.

Even though I felt horrible about the fighting, I got considerable praise from my peers. We were a bunch of privileged white boys in a private Christian school. There wasn't exactly a lot of fighting going on, so this was headline news. Good for me: this would be the last time someone tried to fight me for a while. And I was relieved about that, for I had discovered a rage inside of me that I hadn't known existed. As time went on, the fight inflated my sense of my body's importance as proof of my masculinity. For the first time in my life, my body had won.

Just as formative as my peers' praise was my parents' lack of punishment. My parents were strict, so any absence of discipline was an implicit nod to my behavior. I guess their little karate kid had learned a thing or two after all. Mom and Dad knew I got bullied, so I think they were proud of me. As messed up as it was, winning this fight made me feel better. I started thinking that I was a little more of a man, that I didn't need to be so afraid, that maybe my body wasn't total shit after all.

Chapter 6

MY GIRL

Once I realized I couldn't marry my mom, I had to find my wife. In the folklore of our family lineage, love and marriage happened at a very young age. My grandparents had known each other since kindergarten. Mimi remembered Poppy as "the fat little boy who wouldn't sleep during nap time." Best friends growing up together in the small town of Waveland, Mississippi, they'd eventually realized they were in love and had been married ever since. Dad remembered Mom as the cute new girl with braces, so I understood early on that the one I was supposed to spend the rest of my life with could be right around the corner.

Girls were always nicer to me than boys. I had yet to have any traumatic experiences with girls. There were no girl bullies as far as I could tell. They never called me names, never said I was fat, at least not to my face. I didn't feel pressure to compete or be athletic or wrestle. Girls made me feel good. It was easy to make them laugh too. I imagined that life would be much easier if there were only girls around. I'd also have less competition.

When we lived in Nashville, the country music scene really rubbed off on my mom. She'd blast endless love songs everywhere we went. To this day, I consider myself a recovering country-music listener, but once it's in you, it never really leaves. Every song was about love and the incomplete nature of existence without another person to fill the gaping hole in your heart. My favorite song was by Randy Travis, "Forever and Ever, Amen." If I could only find that person, the one God had made just for me, I would be whole.

When we moved to Atlanta, I met my first girlfriend, Amy, even though I don't think she realized she was my girlfriend. She was a sassy little brown-eyed, curly-haired blonde in my second-grade class. Every day, as soon as I was dropped off at school, I'd search for her, remaining anxious until our reunion in the school yard prior to homeroom. I tried to play it cool, but underneath I stayed nervous. I felt bashful, slow to warm up, until I heard her laugh again. She quickly became my everything.

Amy kissed me on the cheek one time in her backyard under the gazebo, and I was forever hooked. I wanted more. At eight years old, I was officially in love. A window in our house overlooked a busy Atlanta intersection. I would gaze into the clouds and occasionally peer into car windows, searching for Amy and wondering what she was doing, curious if perhaps she was also thinking of me. I would picture her in my mind as I listened to those country songs, convinced she was the only one for me and that we would spend the rest of our lives together.

Amy was the one who told me there was no Santa Claus. I was eating red Jell-O in the school cafeteria. "Your brother's wrong," I defensively declared, unwilling to entertain her blasphemy. She taught me to cheer for the University of Georgia football team. She called me by my full name, Christopher. When she wanted to play the saxophone, I joined band. When she quit, so did I. We would play "truth or dare" on the phone at night, and we'd have to do the dares the next day at school. I always hoped she would dare me to kiss her.

Heartbreak was inevitable; one day across the playground, I saw her kiss another little boy on the cheek. I was crushed. We were just going to be friends now, but there was still hope. Friends could fall in love; everyone knew that. Mimi and Poppy had been friends, and they were happily married. It could be the same for us. I would not give up without a fight. This incident marked a turning point in my romantic pursuits, however. I became less concerned with the prize and more concerned with the competition. Damn those other little boys.

Ashley, a sweet girl in my third-grade class, celebrated her birthday with a pool party, and I was the only boy invited. When it came time to go swimming, I decided to jump in with my shirt on. Ashley's mom came over to me and asked, "Chris, why aren't you taking your shirt off?" I lied and told her that I had a rash on my chest. When she asked to see the rash, I panicked and curtly rebuffed, "My mom told me not to take my shirt off." I was only nine, ashamed of my body, and hyperconscious of what girls found attractive.

Since I spent so much of my early childhood hanging out with girls, I was starting to understand which boys they wanted to kiss and which ones they admired. Being overweight was not mentioned as a desirable trait. Though there were occasional outliers, the general consensus was skinny, athletic, disinterested, and, occasionally, funny. I was in trouble. My only hope would be to play the cute, funny angle and pray for a miracle. I wanted to be attractive, but it was never going to happen so long as I was fat.

In the summer after third grade, my parents bought our house in Sandy Springs, which meant we would be moving again, which meant I wouldn't be going to school with Amy anymore. I was devastated. I don't remember caring about anything or anyone else. Switching schools felt like Amy might as well be dying. Our parents arranged a couple of visits, but it was never the same. I had lost her.

It wasn't long before I found my next victim to fill the void, and she just so happened to live next door to me. Jesse and I were the same age, and though we went to different schools, she was always at the Riverside club. She was kind of a tomboy—a scrappy brunette who liked playing in the dirt and loved animals. She'd do all the stuff the guys would do, and often she'd be the only girl hanging out with the boys. She'd help us build forts. She'd shoot hoops with me in the backyard. We were great friends, best friends even. Our families became friends too. We would go camping together. She was on the swim team with me. We were really close.

Around eleven years old, I started falling for Jesse, and by this time, we both went to Holy Innocents' Episcopal School together. I became possessive. She was mine. I would get incredibly jealous if she showed attention to any other boys. But it wasn't until she started dating my friend Luke that I realized how attracted I was to her. I watched them kiss when we played spin the bottle. It was agony.

For my twelfth birthday, Dad bought me tickets to an Alanis Morissette concert and said I could invite two friends. I had chosen Jesse and Luke a few weeks before they started dating, but they were together by the time of the show. *If there is a hell*, I thought, *it feels like this*. We met up with some other friends for a few minutes during the concert, away from my dad, and I watched as Luke and Jesse kissed at their first opportunity free from adult supervision. I wanted to die.

I stopped hanging out with Jesse and went out of my way to be mean to her. For whatever reason, this made her notice me. Oh, the psychology of little boys and girls. She eventually broke up with Luke, and in a matter of a few weeks after we started hanging out again, she asked me to be her boyfriend. I was thrilled. Later on in life, there would be codes about this sort of thing—"bros before hos," we called it—but not yet. I couldn't wait to betray Luke and start dating Jesse. Her affection validated me in profound ways. It was okay that I was fat; I could still get the girl.

About the same time that we began dating, Jesse started going through puberty. She developed breasts and quickly got the attention of older boys at school. Being her boyfriend started putting me in harm's way. I had unknowingly entered into competition with more guys than I could count. Even if they didn't personally want to date Jesse, they demanded to know why any desirable candidate would want to date me. A significant amount of bullying resulted from Jesse being my girlfriend. She'd be asked all the time, "Why do you date a fat kid?"

One time during after-school car pool, a few eighth graders pinned me down, ripped off my shirt, and started aggressively rubbing my belly, shouting for me to "squeal like a pig." It was the most violated and humiliated I had ever been. All I remember was trying not to cry; I didn't want them to see me upset. Then they would win. One of the boys came over to me afterward and apologized, letting me know that they were just "joking around." I started sobbing and told him to leave me alone. I felt like I'd lost, having shown him how much they hurt me. The most important thing when being bullied was not letting them see any pain.

A couple of months after Jesse and I declared our affection for each other, a few of our friends suggested that we kiss. We began French-kissing, which meant using our tongues. It was weird at first, but we got good at it. We started hanging out after school, French-kissing for hours.

We intentionally picked the longest movies we could to maximize our time together without supervision. There was *Titanic*, which was epically long. We saw it multiple times. I was "the king of the world."

By the time our parents caught on to the steamy nature of our relationship, their efforts were too little, too late. When we were thirteen, Jesse's mom walked downstairs to find her straddling me on the couch with her shirt off. "Time for you to go, Chris," she ordered, pointing to the door. "See you tomorrow." She'd listen in on our phone calls and discover us talking about intimate stuff, like Jesse reading out sex tips from her mom's *Cosmo*. Our moms talked to each other about it, and I was given a couple of sex talks, but they didn't change my thoughts about anything. I was already set on advancing the relationship as much as I could. These were just the games boys played.

Naturally, Jesse's mom started having a big problem with us spending time together. Jesse would tell me the stuff she'd say, like, "How long are you going to date the fat kid?" She did her best to try and split us up. Eventually, she got her wish. We started bickering and broke up. For a while we had an on-and-off type of relationship, but once the breakups start, it's impossible for them to stop. I was mean to her, probably because I was afraid of getting hurt. One day she admitted to kissing another kid. It was our final breakup. I assumed she was into a more physically attractive kind of guy now, and I couldn't help but hate her for it.

I knew from my earliest days of childhood romance that I wouldn't get over Jesse until I found the next girl. That was just the way it worked. A man wasn't right until he found a woman to complete him. She was out there, no doubt; God had created a woman just for me, a soul mate who would make this life worth living. The older I got, the more I understood my incompleteness. Being in love was a part of life, an automatic void that had to be filled with another person. The idea of an external fix for my internal struggle was solidified; I just needed to be patient. God had a plan. It was already written—if I could only have a little faith.

Chapter 7

BINGE-OVERS

Deprivation dominated. I couldn't wait for the weekend. Mom and Dad were strict, so I loved spending nights out at my friends' houses. We would do all the stuff I wasn't allowed to do at home. We would watch R-rated movies and eat unhealthy snacks. It was awesome. Sleepovers were when I got to be bad. Sleepovers were when I got to binge.

The absolute jackpot was when Luke would invite all the Riverside guys over. His mom went to Costco to stock up on groceries, and we would raid their pantry, stuffing as many treats in our pockets and carrying as much as we could down to the basement. I'd make sure to wear my cargo shorts. Once downstairs, I would get to watch the latest Nick Cage shoot-'em-up and gorge my face off. I'd eat so much I'd feel sick. One time, I ate so much I threw up.

There were Gushers, Goldfish, Dunkaroos, chips, candy bars; I never knew what I would get. The suspense was exhilarating. I know I binged at other times, but these are my earliest memories of doing it regularly, planning it, and looking forward to it. I was eleven years old, fully preoccupied with food, constantly on the prowl for the next time I could lose myself. It was full submersion. I was eating the food, and the food was eating me. I got high.

It wasn't long before binge drinking replaced binge eating as the socially preferable activity. The turning point was at Jason's twelfth birthday party. It was the first of many wild birthday celebrations for Jason, since his birthday coincided with New Year's Eve. Even as kids, we knew how to party. Now, instead of Cheetos and Twizzlers, we had beer and liquor. We figured out a way to score alcohol and take it to the sleepover.

I prided myself on being a good little boy in most respects, and I knew drinking was a big no-no. Superscared that anyone was drinking at all, I felt flustered the entire night. The stakes were higher than ever before. Henry was kind of a Goody Two-Shoes, and we discussed our anxiety about drinking and agreed that we would stick together, that we wouldn't imbibe.

Throughout the first hour or so, a couple of the guys got really drunk. Nothing looked right about it. Bobby and Luke started falling over, throwing up, yelling, and crying. Possessed by my total amazement at the mind-altering nature of their experience, I decided I wanted to try. For some illogical reason, it looked like an interesting time. I didn't want to miss out.

I was being bad. Breaking my pact with Henry, to stay strong and not succumb to peer pressure, added an extra thrill to my misbehavior. I sneaked into the bathroom with a couple of little bottles of vodka and chased them with soda. It was like taking medicine. Only a few minutes went by before I started crying, although not because I was particularly drunk. I felt guilty for what I had done. I threw up; the alcohol made me sick. I had betrayed Henry, my parents, and God, but it also felt really good to be such a naughty boy. I was so conflicted.

Everyone besides Henry and me got in big trouble the next week when Jason's neighbors found a trash bag full of empty bottles. Mom and Dad asked me if I drank, and I lied. I cried my little eyes out to them about how bad I felt for partaking in the activities, but I insisted that no alcohol had entered my mouth. Per usual, they believed me. I was already an expert in manipulation, so it wasn't the first time I'd stared them dead in the eye and told blatant mistruths. I lied so much that every cell of my body was convinced. I nearly believed myself.

I started drinking at sleepovers whenever I could. We'd stay up late, hoping for the parents to go to bed. We'd pretend to be asleep, waiting for the obligatory final check-in prior to our anticipated freedom. Drinking was an all-night affair, as we'd spend hours experimenting with our tolerance and flirting with the sunrise. Most of the time, we were just trying not to throw up. We learned the sacred rule of intoxication: "Beer before liquor, never been sicker; liquor before beer, you're in the clear." It was the new deal. There was finally a way to calm down and get out of my head. I was in love.

High school rolled around, so we took our game to the next level. We didn't just stick to alcohol anymore. We started drinking Robitussin. We'd huff upside-down computer duster from Office Depot; it made us sound like Darth Vader. Over and over again, we'd exclaim, "Luuuuke, I am your father." Our laughter bellowed loudly, drowning out any concerns that we might be killing brain cells.

We bought pot from high-school upperclassmen, even though they'd overcharge us at least ten bucks. Mushrooms were the best; we'd take them after school at the park and imagine we were Greek gods high on Mount Olympus. The whole thing felt innocent enough, like an older version of make-believe. I rarely considered any health consequences, possibly because all I ever learned from adults was "Just say no." We'd even take drugs to Young Life, our Christian youth-group retreats. God was better when you were stoned. We would sneak off into the woods outside our cabins and then drop Visine before joining our peers around campfire worship. I'd rationalize it in my mind: *Why would God create drugs if we weren't supposed to partake?*

We'd steal prescription meds from our parents: muscle relaxers, pain-killers, sleeping pills. One time I lay down by my family's pool after taking some Skelaxin and couldn't move my body to go back inside. I stayed there laughing, amused that I could have control over my mind yet none whatsoever over my body. When I woke up after passing out, I was grateful we hadn't gone swimming. Some of us snorted Adderall and made sure our noses weren't covered in blue the next morning. It didn't matter what it was; I wanted to try it.

We'd go garage hopping, hunting in the middle of the night for bottles of alcohol left in open carports. We made pipes out of Coke cans and apples so we could smoke weed without having to keep track of paraphernalia. Our parents were totally clueless; they would take us shopping for snacks to go with our Blockbuster movies, and while they were off in another aisle, we'd steal Coricidin from the pharmacy for our "robo trips."

Ecstasy was hard to get, but I finally scored it from a sketchy dude behind our neighborhood movie theater. I got hustled twice before finding a pill that actually worked. There could have been anything in those round white beans, but I never stopped to consider what was in them or where they came from. Rolling was one of my wilder experiences; it felt like I was falling in love without an object of affection. When Henry's mom picked us up for a sleepover, I was eating a gigantic lollipop and oversharing about how I wished I were better at baseball. I was only fourteen. They had no reason to suspect I was high.

There was some stuff I wouldn't do. I wouldn't use needles, and I wouldn't smoke crack; I'd heard that shit was for hookers and hobos. I misbehaved only on the weekends. During the school week, I was all business. I was voted by my peers to be a representative for the "integrity council." My buddies would come in front of this disciplinary committee, and I'd help them strategize how to get off, coaching them on what they needed to say to sound sincere. I'd teach them how to look the part, how to let everyone know you were a good kid. Adults didn't need much; there wasn't anything difficult about having good manners and maintaining eye contact. My eventual selection to the National Honor Society would throw the grown-ups off my scent for good. "Work hard, play harder" was just how ballers did it.

Chapter 8

CONFIRMATION

My family couldn't figure out what kind of Christians to be. My mom was raised kind of Mormon, and my dad was raised kind of Catholic. We kind of didn't care which cup we used to drink the blood, so long as we stayed thirsty. Mom didn't like the religion of her childhood, but Dad seemed less jaded. I remember Mom talking about God much more than Dad, even though he always led us in prayer. Regardless, they both attributed their straight-and-narrow existence to the grace of God. I was neither straight nor narrow, so religion was just another place I felt strangely distant from my parents.

We were Methodist and then Presbyterian, and then we finally pledged our allegiance to the Roman Catholic Church, which made Mimi happy, but I suspected our conversion was just so it would be easier for me to get into Marist, my high-school alma mater. I asked Mom why we were switching denominations again, and she noted that Dad had grown up Catholic and she felt like she was a Christian above all else. Indeed, they were both good God-fearin', *Fox News*–watchin' Christians in most respects, but I wondered: could you truly love something you were afraid of? Whether by direct communication or inference, I found it important to love the way Jesus taught and scrutinize the details.

I wanted in on one of those divine trips I kept hearing about. To think that I might spend my whole life without God making His presence known to me was depressing. Moses saw a burning bush, angels visited Mary and Joseph, and Noah was inspired to build an ark. I wondered if God would ever decide to talk to me, and I begged Him often in my prayers to choose me as one of His messengers. I searched for Him under every rock and in every errant message of my consciousness. My determination was impeccable though hardly ever fruitful. I longed to drink the same elixir as those chosen before me, and I continued to pray for signs.

The best part about going to a Catholic high school was that I got to study religion every year. The subject fascinated me to no end. I was very contemplative and curious, so the prospect of unanswerable questions and mysterious powers excited me, continually stoking my imagination. I was particularly interested in how people came to understand the gods, since there were so many versions to choose from. Even within my Catholic faith, there were many different ideas of God depending on whom I consulted. The Mormons believed all sorts of crazy stuff. Somebody had to be wrong.

The only thing we could all agree on was the "golden rule": treat people how you would like to be treated. It was a derivative of Jesus's teaching: "love your neighbor as yourself," but a version of it could be found in every religion. Even though we all agreed on this universal tenet, it sent me down a rabbit hole of confusion, one I could never reconcile no matter how hard I tried. I'd never met anyone actually giving this a shot. People seemed more interested in being right than following the rules. The seeds of my future divine delusions were planted in this single commandment, since all I'd ever wanted my entire life was for people to love me the way that I loved them, and nobody could.

When I learned that *Yahweh* meant "I am," my life was changed forever. I considered the name that God had given Himself often, and I interpreted the message to mean that God could never be defined. God became my only coping mechanism that could never fail. The second I imagined lack was the moment I knew I had defined Him. The name with no name—I could see that He existed beyond my rational mind, and I appreciated this immensely, for my rational mind was causing me a great deal of pain. I needed relief from the rules and regulations of a world designed to kill.

Biology taught me that everything was made in the image and likeness of God. Hell, everything was made in the image and likeness of everything, evolving from the same source, so it wasn't that far of a stretch. I had a limited awareness of God in the same way I imagined a cell in my body has a limited awareness of me. I wondered if the universe was just a vast cytoplasmic medium, some infinitesimally small sliver of God's ultimate form. Maybe the sun was like a nucleus of sorts. The more I learned, the more I discovered the magic of God's mysterious design.

Science validated God in profound ways and disproved fundamentalism all the same. I was fortunate to have Catholicism explained as a historical interpretation of scripture, wherein the stories are considered parables and metaphors rather than claims against the well-known facts of modern times. The Garden of Eden story was much more fascinating when it was about human behavior and duality instead of bogus notions that God made humans the way we might bake a cake. I was grateful to have the Bible open to debate and considered subject to human error. It was the only way I could differentiate God from Santa Claus. Metaphor made it real.

The great confusion for me was that some of it was still taken literally, namely the virgin birth, the resurrection of Christ, and the conversion of the Eucharist into the actual body and blood of Jesus. This part flew in blatant opposition to the mythical interpretations usually taught in my religion courses, and my teacher told us we couldn't consider ourselves Catholic while believing that the wine was merely a metaphor. If I were to be truly Catholic, I'd have had to realize that every Sunday I was drinking the actual blood of Christ. This inconsistency opened the crack I'd eventually fall through. I would wonder, "What is the point of miracles?" Perfect love seemed miraculous enough.

In solitude, I sought God out with great fervor, but church was a different story. As a kid, I'd spent more time outside the door of my Sunday-school classes than inside the rooms. Sunday school was like regular school with no consequences and no homework. We would take turns reading the Bible, and I would see how slowly I could read without the teacher commenting. It was the best game in town, since it took a great deal to get one of them to reach the breaking point and instruct, "Read faster." Alex and I would try to hold back our laughter as long as possible, and then crack up once the pressure became irresistible. There was always such great joy to be had at the expense of uptight adults.

Mass was the worst. We were either laughing or falling asleep. Monsignor had the deepest, strangest voice I'd ever heard, with a thick Irish accent to boot. Every time he spoke, I would prod Tyler and Allison, initiating the same tired chain reaction. We would try not to chuckle, which in turn made us chortle, which ended with us being escorted out of the chapel. Sometimes we got Dad too. Perhaps God had a sense of humor and rigged the whole thing this way on purpose. I'd heard that black people stood up and shouted when they felt the Spirit in church; maybe that's what was happening to us.

Eventually, it was time for me to get confirmed. Although my family had converted to Catholicism a few years prior, I now had to make the adult decision to confirm my everlasting faith in the Church. I was fourteen. My misbehavior in a number of forbidden arenas made it hard for me to take the whole thing seriously. I crammed for the occasion the way I would for a vocabulary test. I woke up an hour early on the morning of my confirmation and recited my prayers until they were stored in my short-term faculties, and then I dumped it all on my way out of the ceremony. I remember making a few bullshit confessions to Monsignor, that I had been mean to my siblings and disrespectful to my parents. A few Hail Mary reps did the trick.

The adults hammered home how important the ceremony was, and how those of us being confirmed were now all ready to make a decision for ourselves regarding our faith, but I never seriously considered refusing the sacrament. I believed in Jesus, and that was enough. Nobody really took it all straight without chasing, anyway. The pope didn't even believe in birth control, for crying out loud; I could fudge a little here and there. My parents had already given me the greatest gift any Christian could ever receive: full permission to have a secret, exclusive, and personal relationship with Christ. It was the only confirmation I'd ever need.

Chapter 9

DIET C

I transferred to Marist, a prestigious, private Catholic high school, in ninth grade. The transition wasn't as daunting as some of my earlier ones, mainly because over half of the original Riverside crew was there; Jason, Henry, Alex, and Joe all transferred from Holy Innocents' as well. One of the first things we did as the class of 2003 was attend a nearby camp, a place in north Georgia called High Harbor, for a weekend orientation retreat. There were all sorts of activities—swimming, games, and worship—designed to build rapport and positive peer culture. All I cared about was having fun and avoiding any bullies.

One of the kids working at the camp had begun attending Holy Innocents' the same year that I'd left, so we barely knew each other. I'd heard he had a crush on Jesse; not unlike many other boys at the time, he found his interest in her reason enough to relentlessly bully me. He worked in the cafeteria, and at each meal that weekend, he obnoxiously shouted obscene observations about my body, and the food I was eating, for all my new classmates to hear. He came to my table and asked repeatedly if I was still hungry. He laid it on thick: "Don't worry, Chris, lunch is almost ready. Have no fear, there's plenty of food," implying that I was on the brink of starvation. It was the most relentless and calculated verbal abuse I had ever endured, mainly because he had no quit in him. I was definitely used to kids commenting here and there, but he was particularly dedicated.

At night, when the lights went out in our cabin, I cried myself to sleep. Something snapped in me that weekend. Maybe it was the growing pressure and anxiety of being in a new school. Maybe it was my increasing sexual appetite and intense desire to be attractive. Maybe it was just the last straw. Whatever it was, I became determined to lose weight. I was finally ready to diet. The old me had to die, and a new Chris would need to be born.

I dusted off the diet book that my nutritionist was always trying to get me to read. *Be Fat Free Forever!* was a book written by my allergist, and it was basically a modified version of the popular Atkins Diet. Over the next few months, I would read it cover to cover on multiple occasions. Before, I couldn't be paid to read it. Now, I studied the meal plans, the instructions, and the science behind why the diet worked. Possessed by the pursuit of perfection, I couldn't be stopped.

I became a machine. My friends used to call me "Big C," but not anymore. I became "Diet C." Now, I would be best known for my constant dieting habits and nutritional restrictions.

I read that body mass index, or BMI, was a terrible predictor for body shape composition, so I asked my parents to buy me a scale that included body-fat percentage. I measured myself immediately upon awakening, right after I peed, naked, every morning, like clockwork. This was the right way to use the scale, to make sure you got accurate and consistent results. My scale was so sick; it would automatically chart my progress with a graph by weight and body-fat percentage. As long as the numbers were going down, I was happy.

I began intercepting my dad's *Men's Health* and *Men's Fitness* magazines, even subscribing to a version for teens, called *MH-18*; I studied these subscriptions with evangelical zeal. I bought a book on weight lifting advertised in one of the magazines. I read it front to back, learning about the science behind bodybuilding, correct form, and how to combine different exercises to maximize results. I started creating workout routines for each day of the week, and I'd draft each one with the sort of ardor you might expect from little kids writing letters to Santa. I was meticulous to no end, and excited for each new challenge. The burn in my muscles was direct confirmation that I was doing it right. It all hurt so good.

I started borrowing my parents' credit card to buy supplements at GNC. My personal trainer introduced me to ephedrine, a drug commonly found in diet pills, and then, when the stuff was banned as an illegal substance, I switched to similar products without skipping a beat. I alternated between Xenadrine and Hydroxycut, hoping not to build a tolerance to either one of them. I took these diet pills in the morning when I woke up and thirty minutes before workouts in the afternoon. I began taking an additional supplement at night before bed that was supposed to enhance muscle growth. I added creatine to my preworkout routine. I befriended a GNC employee and asked him to give me whatever was the closest thing to steroids. We agreed that anabolics were unnecessary given the plethora of legal options available.

I started drinking protein shakes around the clock. I'd consume a gram of protein per pound of body weight in powder alone. I took whey protein powder if I wanted a quick hit, and I had an egg protein powder to take before bed for a slower uptake. I started making a shake to drink in the middle of the night, so my body would never go more than four hours without it, but after a few days of waking up at 2:00 a.m., I decided that was too obsessive. Instead, I drank raw eggs as a nightcap, hoping that would be sufficient until morning.

For breakfast, I would eat leftover meat from the night before or scrambled eggs and a protein shake. I packed lunch for myself each morning: two "protein rolls" consisting of deli meat, cheese, lettuce, and mustard; a low-carb protein bar; and a bag of beef jerky. For dinner, I asked my mom to accommodate my dieting needs, which required a lean protein, a nonstarchy vegetable, and a side salad. I drank a protein shake before and after my weight-lifting sessions. Protein was all I ate; the other nutrients would work themselves out.

From *Be Fat Free Forever!*, I deduced that binge eating was basically allowed for one hour, once a week. The medical science indicated that the insulin response, the metabolic process responsible for converting sugar to body fat, would be minimal if "cheating" were confined to a short, infrequent period of time. I started planning my attack and binging accordingly. Most of the time, I just held out as long as I could. Then when

I would break the diet, I would gorge myself on sweets, starches, bread, and other carbs as quickly as possible. Alcohol wasn't a part of the diet, so I'd often count my binge-drinking episodes as my cheat for the week. Eventually, my cheats went on longer than planned. Monday through Friday, you could find me in the gym, and then Friday night through Sunday became my designated binge times, wherein a mixture of alcohol, drugs, and sugar provided enough release to make me want to get back on the wagon come Monday.

My parents were mostly oblivious to the level of disorder I had developed, and they were blinded by their pride in their once-fat son's miraculous transformation. As with many compulsions, addictions, and destructive behaviors, lying was a huge part of it. As the saying goes, the best lies include an element of truth. They knew I was dieting and exercising, but that was encouraged. They didn't know I was stealing money to buy supplements at GNC. They thought I just took multivitamins. They didn't know how much protein powder I was consuming. I hid it from them. I kept my diet pills and supplements stashed in my closet. In their minds, I'd just finally, after all these years of struggling with my weight, discovered some self-discipline and motivation.

I made sure to flirt with the carbohydrate-restricted fasting state of ketosis as often as possible. I eventually lost about 70 pounds, going from 240 to under 170. I was pleased to be within the normal parameters for BMI at my yearly physical. I was finally healthy. My pediatrician asked me what I had done, and I told him about my dieting strategies. He commended me for my effort and discipline. "Keep it up," he cheered.

My fitness and dieting habits continued to ramp up. The whole thing became something like an inverse addiction. If I did it, I felt good about myself and everything seemed okay for the most part. If I wavered at all, by cutting a workout short or eating a piece of bread, I felt like a complete failure, debilitated until I could string together a few days of perfection. The solution? Just keep it up. Just keep dieting. Just be perfect, until the weekend; then catch my breath and do it all again.

Chapter 10

SIZE MATTERS

I'd had a generally bad feeling about showing my naked body since I was a kid. This ubiquitous malaise included taking my shirt off to go swimming, but there was an extra emphasis on keeping private parts private. I knew that my penis was secret to me and that people kept their penises and vaginas hidden at all times, except to take a bath or go potty, and whenever possible, I tried my best to follow the rules.

The first time I considered the fact that my penis might be different from other boys' was when a childhood pal showed me his uncircumcised member while we peed together. When I told him that his penis looked weird, he informed me, "No, it doesn't. Yours looks weird. You had yours chopped off!" Terrified, I ran to my parents to solicit their support in the matter. They gave me some minimal explanation about how normal it was to be circumcised, but that some boys weren't. Come to find out, my first cosmetic procedure occurred in the delivery room.

My original orgasm was quasi-accidental, a prepubescent tour de force courtesy of my parents' bathtub Jacuzzi jets around the age of ten. These aquatic adventures were already plenty delightful, but I never imagined the ecstasy my body was capable of until summiting this semenless peak. And so, on that rainy afternoon, with my penis pressed firmly against this perfectly concentrated mixture of air and water, I had finally arrived. Sex became my ultimate principle, the guiding force behind my every neurosis.

My parents and the clergy taught me that sexual pleasure was forbidden until marriage, so my self-love was top-secret material; I didn't talk about it to anyone, lest I be damned. Alex and Joe even told me that a nun had announced to their class, "Every time you masturbate, an angel loses its wings!" This secret love affair with my penis was a lustful one, the kind made more enchanted by prohibition. I would sneak into private, whether bathing or pretending to poop, and tend to my lover, my precious source of infinite pleasure. I couldn't wait to include another in my games, and I just prayed God would forgive me.

There wasn't really one particular event responsible for my distorted view of my penis; it was a confluence of a few things. For one, I hadn't lost weight yet, and the great deal of adipose tissue surrounding my pickle presented an opportunity for it to entirely disappear, shrinking into oblivion as it occasionally went the way of innie belly buttons and scared turtle heads. I noticed it got particularly tiny when I exercised or if it was chilly outside. Swimming laps in a cold pool would nearly reassign me.

I went through puberty after all my friends, so while I noticed other boys increasing in size in locker rooms and at sleepovers, I was behind. One time, while I was sporting my jockstrap in the locker room, Jason shouted out that it looked like I had a vagina. It was humiliating.

My predicament was exacerbated at my newest bestie Sam's house. During a sleepover, Jason and Henry struck up a drunken argument about who had a bigger dick, which eventually led them to go into separate rooms to get erect and then come back to have us all decide the wiener. Jason looked to me like he had a third leg. All I knew was that I would have lost to both of them. I leaned over to Bobby and asked, "Is Henry's small?" Bobby replied, "Not at all, dude, Jason is just huge." *Thank God*, I thought to myself.

Also, I was more of a "grower" than a "shower." As a kid, when I was in situations where my penis would show, I would try to get aroused in order to offset this effect. I became very bashful about simple tasks such as peeing in standing urinals. If there was no guard between my toilet and the next, I would go into the stalls instead. I would rub my penis before going up to bathroom urinals in case someone were to witness my inadequacy.

I would tug on it before taking off my towel in the showers and corner myself away from others when I changed in gym class.

My obsession grew so bad that I actually didn't believe my penis had grown at all through puberty, when actually it had. One time, a study of average penis size was featured in *Men's Health*. I was all over it. The study revealed that my erection was average in both length and girth. I didn't believe the study. Perhaps I wasn't okay with average.

In another fitness magazine, I read about how you could increase the size of your penis by losing weight, that extra pounds of fat made the penis appear smaller. This was just another reason to get more ripped. My weight loss continued to gain importance in every aspect of my life. I was convinced that my entire self-worth, sexuality, and eventual marriage would all be contingent on my ability to decrease my body-fat percentage and increase my penis size.

I was getting so twisted that I was ready to talk to my pediatrician about it. I thought about my penis size all the time. When my parents scheduled me for a checkup, I began working up the courage to ask the pediatrician about his thoughts on the matter. After he did his usual routine, which included gripping my balls and telling me to cough to the side, I asked him plainly, "Doc, is my penis going to get any bigger?" I couldn't believe I was asking him, but the pain was getting unbearable. He looked uncomfortable and tersely replied, "No."

There was, of course, the porn issue. When I was in early adolescence, my friends and I would get dropped off at the mall to hang out. There was a bookstore there, where we would steal pornographic magazines. It was always a surprise what we'd get, since they were covered in black plastic. Whoever did the actual stealing got to keep the magazine. After a few turns at playing the accomplice, I was ready to get my own. I was terrified but acted anyway, and this one magazine would be a mainstay in my masturbating habits for years to come.

At the back of the magazine were a number of advertisements, including one for a pill that promised to add inches to your penis. I stole my parents' credit-card number and ordered a bottle. I checked the mail every day as soon as I got home from school, hoping to intercept the package. I was successful. My pills of "Longitude" had arrived. In the package were special instructions. It wasn't as simple as just popping a pill. The directions, which I wanted to follow perfectly in order to ensure optimal results, included some pretty extreme measures of self-abuse. I didn't think twice about it.

In addition to taking the pills, for about ten minutes I had to perform two different exercises. First, I had to tug my flaccid penis in a circular motion to "stretch" the tissue. Second, I was instructed to "jelq" my semi-erect penis in order to increase the size of the blood compartments, which meant repeatedly milking my dick like a cow udder. The jelqing resulted in horrible pain and bruising. It never occurred to me that I was undergoing a form of self-harm. I did this twice a day for a month before ordering another bottle. There was no noticeable change to my penis size, but it certainly remained black-and-blue.

My dad discovered the second bottle of Longitude before I had a chance to get to it first. I was lifting weights in our home gym, and Dad approached me with the package. I'm not sure if it said anything on the bottle about enhancing size, but for whatever reason, Dad thought it was a performance-anxiety issue. While I had indeed excused myself a couple of times to rub one out in the bathroom during my hookups with Jesse, this was not my primary concern. He tried his best to normalize premature ejaculation, but it was an uncomfortable discussion and didn't result in me confessing how difficult a time I was having. I wouldn't tell him that I was scared my penis was too small, even though my thoughts were increasingly becoming drastically distorted.

I started to imagine I'd been born a hermaphrodite. I considered there might have been a complication with my circumcision. I wondered if God was punishing me in some way. I thought maybe God wanted me to be a priest, so he made my dick so small that no woman would ever enjoy sex with me. I was getting supersick. This coincided with my increased drinking and drug behavior. I was afraid to pursue sexual relations because of what a girl might think about my penis. I thought that I wouldn't be able to get married. I wondered if Jesus had a small penis, and that was why he didn't marry Mary Magdalene. I began to research penis-enlargement procedures, but following through would have required me actually admitting to someone that I had a small dick, and frankly, I would rather have died.

My size concerns and anxiety around nudity played a huge part in my decision to eventually quit sports entirely. There were other reasons I stopped, such as that I had asthma and allergies, that I was unathletic, and that I wanted to do other things with my time, like get stoned and lift weights, but there was definitely an acute awareness that we were starting to shower naked together, and I was mortified. I already knew of a few guys who had nicknames based on their penis size or shape, and I wasn't about to be one of them.

As I transitioned to Internet porn, my fixation grew worse. The more porn I watched, the more convinced I became of my inadequacy. I started thinking that I had the smallest penis in the world. I searched for small penises on the Internet to make sure mine was bigger. I suspected I had a micropenis, even when my measurements clearly placed me outside of this diagnosis. Every joke told in a movie or a comedy routine deepened my isolation. I scoured average-penis-size studies. No amount of information could change the way I felt about it.

Porn perpetuated my problem, but I was far too close and perversely secretive to see what was happening in my mind. The videos showed a lot of different women and various female features, with great variation in breast size, nipple shape, vaginas, and bodies. As for the guys, some were skinny and some were muscular, but they all shared one thing in common: a humongous cock. It was obviously the only necessary ingredient in porn and, as far as I was concerned, in pleasing a woman. I was screwed.

One of my religion classes in high school was called "Choices," and during the course, we would have the famous sex talk. Boys and girls wrote down questions for the opposite sex, to be read anonymously. I don't remember anything except that one of the boys asked, "Does penis size matter?" A couple of things were going on for me here. One, I hadn't asked the question, so at least one other boy was curious about this. Two, if one boy had been brave enough to write this, how many other boys, like me, were interested but not willing to ask?

I took the class with my high-school crush, Chloe. When that question was read out loud, she leaned over to me, and I looked into those big brown eyes as she insisted, "It doesn't matter at all." I wanted to believe her, but I couldn't. By this time, I was so entrenched in my insecurities that, when the other girls in the class began echoing Chloe's opinion, all I heard was a bunch of girls lying. They were saying that size didn't matter just to make us feel better. I told myself, "Most of these girls haven't had sex yet, so they aren't authorities on the matter." I imagined that Chloe thought I had a small penis, and that was why she was going out of her way to comfort me.

More time went on, and I kept getting sicker. I stopped wearing certain mesh gym shorts. I was afraid someone would see the outline of my dick. I feared any clothes that would possibly reveal "the bulge." Bathing suits were particularly problematic, because of the suction effect that occurred when you first got out of the water. I'd wait until no one was looking to get out of the pool. I was lucky board shorts were cool; they had that strip of Velcro barricading my potential embarrassment.

My Christian upbringing helped in some ways, because sex was such a forbidden activity. I used this as a convenient excuse to put off thoughts about sexual intercourse. I wasn't as afraid of oral sex, having already somehow received a couple of drunken blow jobs, although I needed to be superwasted for those, otherwise I definitely would've been too anxious. I became a self-proclaimed virgin, proud to inform others that I was saving myself for my wife. It didn't consciously occur to me that masturbation, pornography, and oral sex were also sinful. I was picking and choosing what worked for my distorted mind. I was a good boy, a good Christian, and nothing was going to change that for me— not my dick, not anything.

Chapter 11

NO HOMO

For a kid growing up in the conservative Christian South, the term *gay* didn't really have much to do with sex. Music, clothing, foods, mannerisms, beliefs were all potentially gay areas. Before things were gay, *sissy* was the code word for girly stuff boys shouldn't do. Like most of my peers, I was raised with pretty clear ideas about the differences between boys and girls, so when the verbiage switched from *girly* and *sissies* to *gay* and *fags*, it wasn't hard to keep up. The most dangerous gay terrain was the inner emotional landscape of boys. To show any emotion other than anger was supergay, a tough rule for this sensitive boy.

Even though we used *gay* and *faggot* as derogatory terms for one another, there wasn't much awareness that we were expressing disdain for a group of people. We called one another these names to exert a kind of peer pressure for masculine conformity. Sometimes a kid was gay for crying. Sometimes a dude was a fag because he liked a song by the Backstreet Boys. I remember guys getting teased just for liking Popsicles because, I guess, they looked like they were giving a blow job. It was somewhat predictable, but the strictness of the gay rules depended on each person's consideration of what ultimately defined a man. It might be as straightforward as not dressing in drag or as obscure as not drinking from a straw.

My penis was always getting me into trouble. I had some ideas about homosexuality, but I never spent much time considering my own

categorization until I had already engaged in some minor same-sex explo-
ration. I thought of these episodes as accidents; one night I was playing
"truth or dare," and the next thing I knew, I was being dared to touch
penises with a random kid in my neighborhood. The next day I was trying to forget it ever happened, but then it happened another time with a
different kid. I didn't pay much attention to it. I hadn't even gone through
puberty yet. But then in high school, once there was suddenly such intense
hatred for homosexuality, I felt ashamed and scared and confused.

My early adolescent sexual activity was all innocent enough, but once
I began learning more about what it actually meant to be gay, outside of
taste in music and emotional disposition, I was terrified of my sexual orientation. I even heard you could go straight to hell! Because I had already
been sexually active with girls, I was even more confused. Bisexuality
wasn't an option. You were either gay or straight, and you had to pick
your team.

When it came to the criteria for being gay, I knew I met many of the
fringe requirements. I liked the Dixie Chicks. I cried watching *Free Willy*.
I genuinely enjoyed the company of girls. I sucked at sports. If the gay
police were going to interrogate any of my friends, I would no doubt be
one of the first suspects called in for questioning. And yet, as much as I
considered that I might be gay, I really loved girls. I had huge crushes on
them. I masturbated to them. I was positive that I was sexually attracted
to women.

I started to consider that my sexual appetite was just very high. I liked
being touched. I liked touching myself. I thought that perhaps my same-
sex activity was just an expression of my high sex drive. I wondered if I
was possibly an entirely unique type of sexuality, that I might be "auto-
sexual," some rare breed that could be sexually aroused no matter the cir-
cumstance. Alone in my confusion, I was sure I was fatally and uniquely
flawed, growing in my doubts as to whether I'd ever be truly loved. There
was no one I felt comfortable talking to about my sexuality. It was my
cross to bear.

By the time I got to high school, it had been a couple of years since I'd
engaged in any questionable activity. I remember making the decision that
I preferred girls to boys, and there was little doubt in my mind that this was
true. I especially only cared to kiss girls—that is, if you didn't count those

steamy autoerotic practice sessions pressed against my bedroom mirror. It wasn't hard to sublimate any homosexual impulses. However, the looming possibility that I was gay remained, and I consciously guarded against all behavior that might be misconstrued as anything less than alpha macho.

At a couple of sleepovers, I heard rumors of a few same-sex incidents between friends that frightened me a great deal. One of my classmates had reportedly gotten drunk and given a hand job to another classmate, and everyone at school was talking about it. I had a slipup shortly thereafter, in ninth grade, when I got drunk and let one of my friends jack my dick for a few seconds. I immediately became fearful that I would be implicated in all of the gay accusations flying around campus. I feared the inquisition. It was the last same-sex encounter I'd ever have. I decided I wasn't gay; I just liked it when someone else played with my junk. To be gay, you had better be damn sure, because it sure seemed like a hell of a lot of trouble.

God was doing this to me. I couldn't tell if He wanted me to be a priest or not. I considered that Jesus might have been gay, and that was why He never got married. I mean, the dude died a thirty something-year-old virgin, right? I was trying to piece it all together. My body, my penis, and my sexuality were God's domain, and there was a reason for everything. Sex was of paramount importance, and God was like a judgmental Peeping Tom when it came to issues of Eros. I questioned whether he'd ever forgive me for my early sexual blunders.

My desire to be admired and attractive included a subconscious effort to display masculine traits. Although I wasn't totally aware of the connection at the time, my aspirations to be muscular and strong seemed to be caught up in my insatiable hunger for the masculine ideal. If I was enough of a beast, no one could question my manhood. Included in my drive for physical perfection was an incessant pursuit of emotional stoicism. Repudiating emotion, I refused to feel a thing, except in front of my parents, but even then, my tears were only in moments of total despair and dysregulation, and then I'd talk about something trivial to mask the true source of my pain. I was an absolute mess, convinced I was the only person capable of such incomprehensible suffering.

So here I was, a young adolescent male trying hard to be as manly as possible. I would do anything to play the part. My muscular body was like my costume, and my macho bravado, my mask. The benefits of a bigger, badder body seemed endless. I would be more attractive to girls, more socially accepted, and less likely to endure ridicule from other guys. I suited up, determined to be bulletproof. They wouldn't be able to touch me. Any diffidence or perceived imperfection was fuel for the fire in my desperate desire to burn up any and all obstructions to masculinity.

Chapter 12

ANGELS AND DEMONS

Sam was my only close friend who wasn't a member of the original Riverside crew. I had known him since basketball, but we became best friends on the Holy Innocents' middle-school baseball team. I was devastated when I didn't make the baseball team my first year, since every one of my friends did except for me. Luckily, Coach let me practice with them and named me the official team manager. Sam loved baseball, and he was generous, giving me tips, teaching me to grip the ball with just my fingers, and coaching me on how to keep my swing compact.

My parents encouraged me to work really hard and try to make the team the following year; they even paid for private lessons in the batting cage. I applied myself and it paid off. In eighth grade, Jason and Henry played on junior varsity, Alex and Joe had already transferred to Marist, and Bobby and Luke chose soccer, but Sam and I were together, and we had a blast. I hit at the bottom of the order, but thanks to him and my coaches, I ended up driving in the most RBIs that season. It was the highlight of my tiny sports career.

Sam's dad was a lawyer, and he kept a minifridge packed with beer. When I stayed at his house, we'd sneak two bottles downstairs and drink them together. Sam wanted to be a lawyer, just like his dad. He had a sharp wit and gregarious presence, which we believed would help him in the courtroom one day. And I could relate to wanting to emulate one's father.

Sam was a pretty eccentric kid. When he started driving, he would crank up the floor heat of his black 4Runner and roll the windows down, even though it was winter. He wore an old baseball cap everywhere, putting it on immediately after a shower, before his hair was even dry. This might have been because we all gave him shit for rocking a butt cut the longest. He was fun and kind of cocky but a little bashful too, in the sort of way that accidentally lets you know it's okay to be yourself. He reminded me of Chandler Bing, the facetious, slightly neurotic character from *Friends*. Even though all of us except Sam and Bobby transferred out of Holy Innocents' for high school, our friendships only grew stronger.

Early one morning in January during my sophomore year of high school, I suddenly woke up to the phone ringing. It was too early for someone to be calling, very out of the ordinary. After a couple of minutes, I picked up the phone to see what was going on, and my mom was quick to hang up. "I'll talk to you soon," she hastily declared to the unknown caller. I knew something was up.

A few minutes later, Mom entered my room and sat down next to me on the bed. Her face was red, and she was crying. Through quivering lips she blurted it out: "Sam died last night in a car accident. I'm so sorry, Chris."

Shock went over my body. I burst into tears. "This can't be happening," I sobbed, clinging tight to her. Just a few weeks earlier, my classmate and tennis partner, Isaac, had died suddenly of a brain aneurism. *What the fuck is going on?* I wasn't even through grieving over Isaac and now this. Death was everywhere.

Sam loved cars, and his particular obsession had been the vehicle his dad had recently purchased for himself, one he'd begged his dad to buy, the Jaguar XKR. His dad had let him borrow the car to return some Blockbuster videos about a quarter mile from their house. I heard Sam had driven the car only once before. I could've thrown a baseball from their block to the store—that's how close it was; but Sam decided to take an alternate route in order to let her rip. When they found the car wrecked against a tree along the winding road back to his home, Sam was already gone. He'd been speeding and lost control. My parents and I drove by the site to try to understand what had happened. The XKR was still there, flipped over high up on a neighbor's lawn. I studied the scene, needing to feel the impact, stunned.

The Riverside gang visited Holy Innocents' that day to grieve with our former schoolmates. We all cried in the dimly lit hallways. I remember it raining, but that may just be a figment of the hurt. I felt as if death were a mere breath away. A poster of the Jaguar was taped to the inside of his locker, a difficult and ominous sign of his love for the vehicle that killed him. Boys and their car obsessions—we could all relate too well.

Grieving for Sam was much more difficult than grieving for Isaac had been. I had been closer with Sam, and because we'd gone to different high schools, my Marist classmates weren't grieving with me as much. When Isaac died, the whole school had cried for days. In every classroom, we'd turned out the lights and listened to music as kids laid their heads down and sobbed through tissue boxes. When Sam died, all my sorrow from Isaac carried over, and I was absolutely distraught, so much so that I found it difficult to finish a full cry. When Isaac died, I'd cried my eyes out for days. When Sam died, I felt dissociated, like I couldn't embody such great levels of pain. I went numb.

There's no describing how sad I felt for Sam's and Isaac's families. Their parents wound up becoming friends, since I guess they could understand what they were each going through like no one else could. Sam's mom called to ask if I would be a pallbearer, and I had no idea what she meant, so I asked my parents to explain it to me. I found out a few of us were going to carry Sam's dead body into church during the funeral. Later, we would help bury him at the cemetery. I felt nauseous. *What the fuck, God?* I demanded. Everyone told me not to curse at God, but it felt good to let Him know I was pissed.

The wake was the most difficult part. Sam's casket was open. I remembered his face, full of life, how he was always joking around. Now his face was dim and expressionless. His body lay still and stagnant. It was official. Sam was dead.

We couldn't look for long, and all of us decided to get out of there at the first opportunity. Because of the extraordinary circumstances, my folks allowed me to go to a friend's house to grieve, even though I was grounded. By this time, I was almost always grounded. I was hardly the only one drinking, but I was usually the only one in trouble, because I was the only one who couldn't call my parents without talking in tongues. I was always sorry during the multihour epic conversations with my parents that followed, crying and promising them that I would fare better the next time, but I had lost the power of choice in the matter. I needed to get fucked up way more than I needed my parents.

The night of Sam's wake, all of us drank beer together, laughed, cried, and recited fond memories of our dear comrade as we did our best to cope with the painful reality of life's fragility. Death was the only time men were allowed to cry. I felt scared, the kind of fear that shuts off the senses. I didn't want to die.

My parents always waited up for me, which was partially why I would get grounded so much. But that night, when I got home, even though he could tell what I'd been up to, Dad didn't punish me for drinking. He just looked at me, tired and sad, gave me a long hug, and told me he loved me. "Go get some sleep," he said. It was the only time he ever gave me an exemption.

The funeral marked a poignant moment in my religious journey. Sam's favorite band was the Beatles, and "Let It Be" played in our procession, though instead of "words of wisdom," all I heard were words of confusion. One of our middle-school teachers, an Episcopalian priest, led the service. Supposedly Sam had given the guy a hard time in his religion courses, so some of us knew he wasn't a great candidate to give our friend a proper valediction. He was also my adviser on the integrity council. I didn't think the holy man was so bad, but he did have a tinge of righteous uptightness.

The priest devoted the funeral service to a long-drawn-out theological and existential query on whether or not Sam was in heaven. It took me a few minutes to realize what was happening. He talked about how we didn't know God's will or determination on matters of the afterlife, how all we could do was hope to see our loved ones there one day. "We simply cannot know where Sam is right now," he repeated. I hadn't pegged him for the vengeful type, but this was messed up. Perhaps he actually believed Sam might be condemned to hell. I don't know.

I was in such a delicate emotional space that I wasn't sure if I was even hearing him right. All the pallbearers were sitting in a pew up front. We stirred in our seats, tears streaming down our faces, trying to understand how this could happen, why God would take our friend, and then this bullshit. My buddies and I looked at one another between subtle wipes of our handkerchiefs, silently affirming, "Yes, this is ridiculous." We all partook in a collective exhalation as he finally stopped talking.

To everyone's surprise, Sam's dad wanted to give the eulogy. He was getting slammed in the media for letting his son drive such a fast and expensive car. Sam was the first Atlanta teenager to die in a car wreck in 2001, so there was an inordinate amount of media coverage. The *Atlanta Journal-Constitution* ran the story of Sam's death, citing how he'd had his license for only three months. Then, right below, on the same page, they ran an op-ed about spoiled rich kids and the parents who let them drive fancy cars.

Just seeing Sam's dad up there at the podium wrenched my soul as I considered my own father's love. He talked about how he'd done his best to be a role model for Sam, but said that there was so much he himself admired in his son. He listed Sam's many attributes, including his analytical and discerning mind, no doubt one of the qualities that had so perturbed the priest. He took out Sam's weathered hat, the one Sam had worn every day, and put it on his head. My soul shook. During his brilliant homage to his newly deceased son, he made it clear that Sam was in heaven, emphatically informing the packed crowd, "I *know* where my son is."

The priest's heartless homily, and the beautiful response by Sam's dad, opened the floodgates of skepticism regarding the Church and her chosen officials. It marked the beginning of my dissent. I didn't stop believing in God, but I was sure as hell that none of those fuckers were going to tell me anything about Him. With my opinions influenced by recent revelations of sexual abuse allegations within the Church, I began looking at priests as if they might be the devil himself in disguise.

When the service ended, we buried Sam in a cemetery around the corner from my house. Over the next few years, I would go back there often to talk to him about my difficulties, trying to find some sort of closure. Desperate to understand, I didn't want to be mad at God. *Please, please help me see Your will*, I'd tearfully plead. I felt so close to Sam's ghost. I could feel him comfort me. He'd visit me in my dreams and tell me everything was going to be okay.

It wouldn't be long before I'd start attending Sam's grave to drink and smoke pot with him. I'd pour out some of my liquor, a sign of respect I'd seen in movies and rap videos. I'd rip the bowl as hard and deep as my lungs would allow, exhaling the smoke, whispering, "This is for you, bro." I attributed omniscience to Sam's spirit and shared all of my struggles with him. He was my guardian angel. I asked him what he thought about Jesus, and he'd tell me. They were good buddies up in heaven.

There were times here and there that we would all talk about Sam, but pretty soon it stopped. It was just too sad. We were all hurting; Joe even got Sam's initials tattooed on his ankle, but I figured my parents would kill me if I got a tattoo. My dad encouraged me to use Sam's life as inspiration, to live my own life to the fullest in his honor. It seemed I had something slightly different in mind. I began drinking and drugging more frequently, a conscious response to the imminent threat of death. "Eat, drink, and be merry, for tomorrow we die," became my favorite line from Dave Matthews, by way of the Bible, a motto for my newly adopted live-in-the-moment philosophy.

Chapter 13

WHITE WATER

The party was primed, ready to go full-time. Occasional after-school smoke sessions and weekend booze binges would be replaced with the day in, day out daze of summer. Fresh off our sophomore year of high school, we were ready to kick off our season of freedom. It had been an eventful school year; I was a member of both the National Honor Society and the French Honor Society, and my reputation for being the one somehow balancing all this partying with good grades was cemented. I played the part well. Looking back on it, my excellent GPA and zero demerits were likely the only factors keeping my parents from sending me to rehab.

We had all started driving that year, which made engaging in illicit activity simpler. I could stash drugs and alcohol in the brand-new 2001 Ford Sport Trac my parents had bought me for my sixteenth birthday. I no longer had to hide in basements to hook up with girls, hoping our parents wouldn't interrupt. Now, we could just get it on in the back of my truck, provided I was fucked up enough not to have a panic attack or bust a load inside my colorful khaki shorts. It was my golden era, when I was no longer fat and not so far gone in my addictions as to be entirely debilitated. I was stoked for summer and the promise of more.

It was time for me to take my shirt off again. Even though I had lost a great deal of weight, I was still incomprehensibly self-conscious. My buddies and I decided to take a day trip to White Water, the local aquatic theme park for little kids and big rednecks. There were slides, lazy rivers, wave pools, rides, and all sorts of obstacle courses where Georgia's finest gathered for innocent, wet-and-wild fun. We thought it'd be a good idea to get fucked up in order to enhance our experience. Everything was better drunk and high. I liked altering my consciousness mostly because it made me forget about my enormous nipples and unsightly stretch marks. Going out of my mind helped me forget about my body.

My Sport Trac came in handy. There was a secret compartment, for housing tools and emergency supplies, where I stashed some weed and vodka for our excursion. Once we got to the parking lot, we started tailgating the way you might see sports fans preparing for a play-off game. We had folding chairs, coolers, and food ready for our day in the sun. We spent a little over an hour preparing for entry. My Ford had a cover over the truck bed, and Alex and I crawled in there to hotbox the space. I rolled out, high as a kite, ready to drink up. A flask of Smirnoff was enough to get the job done back then.

Even at sixteen, I was just in the middle of puberty and had only small patches of hair under my arms. My friends sometimes called me "baby face." I could've passed for twelve. I was absolutely hammered as we walked down the long pier-like structure that seemed to stretch forever up to the park entrance. I could hardly put one foot in front of the other, but it was a fun game to play, trying to walk straight while maintaining a straight face. The guy in the ticket booth didn't ask any questions, so I was in the clear.

I don't know if there was a delay in my drunkenness, or if dehydration and excessive sun exposure eventually got to me, but the rest of my White Water experience is pretty blurry, punctuated by the memory-less void of my first blackouts. We went over to the lily pads, these big rubbery floats that formed an obstacle course across roped monkey bars. The objective: make it to the other side. I fell off the first one and barely missed hitting my head on the edge of the pool from whence I'd come. Then, like an awkward baby seal, I tried to flop onto the next lily pad with no success as the lifeguard whistled for me to swim to safety. I was lucky I made it out, demonstrating the least sufficient skill to prevent the lifeguard from coming to my aid.

Stubbing my toe on our way to the Bahama Bob Slide, I announced, "Dude, our epidermises are the same, man," drunkenly slurring to my buddies, spouting off random biology facts from my most recent exam. When we got to the long, winding line leading to our ride, I tried to climb a wooden wall to cut ahead. A security guard stopped me upon my ascent. "Son, please walk around to the entrance," he sternly ordered. When I turned around to reply, "Shooo shorry offisher," he acted embarrassed, apologized to my friends, and encouraged them to help me find my way. He thought I was disabled. He wasn't entirely wrong.

Up next was the gigantic wave pool, ever populated by a sea of people floating on inner tubes. Every few minutes, the waves would turn on, and it was most fun to free swim in the deep end. After nearly drowning for a few rounds, I started feeling sick, so I made my way over to the endless row of poolside lawn chairs. I sat down and hadn't even leaned back before I threw up all over myself. Even when I was finished vomiting, I continued to dry heave. Some adults swarmed the area and quickly realized that this kid was totally wasted.

Medical officers and security guards got me onto a wheelchair and escorted me to an ambulance. The last thing I remember is riding in the wheelchair through the park as a bunch of parents and children watched me hit my first bottom: sixteen years old, drunk and stoned, at an amusement park, while my parents thought I was spending the day soaking up rays and riding slides for some innocent fun with my friends. I was gaining clarity faster than I wanted to admit. I was out of control, and once I started drinking, I was rarely able to stop.

When I came to in the hospital bed, I opened my eyes to see my parents' crying faces looking back at me, their silhouettes blurry in the foreground against whiteout walls and bright fluorescent lighting. God could've killed me in that moment, and I wouldn't have argued with Him. I felt about as worthy as a fresh piece of dog shit in the middle of a busy sidewalk. They didn't need to say a word, but we talked anyway. Cue the waterworks. I was sorry, like I always was, and I was grounded, again, this time for the whole summer.

Since all discipline was failing at this point, my folks decided my condition warranted professional help. Prior to the White Water event, they'd been hoping I was just experimenting, caught in a phase I would soon grow out of, but now they were appropriately disturbed. I went to see a prominent psychologist, the adolescent addiction expert in Atlanta. He assessed my parents' concerns and had me fill out some questionnaires, to which I responded with about five percent of the truth. He then placed me into group counseling with a bunch of fellow fuckups. When the other kids shared about their drug and alcohol experiences, I related to their actual substance use, but I definitely didn't relate to the way they talked about it. They used a lot of slang and seemed to be bragging. I was ashamed of my behavior. I wasn't like them.

No matter how much my substance abuse resembled that of my troubled peers, I found ways to distance myself, convinced that my outstanding academic success and conservative Christian beliefs merited special treatment. I clung even tighter to my superiority with every suggestion that I might be like them. They told war stories about popping skittles, skipping class, and running away from home. If you asked me, they were either trying too hard or not trying hard enough. Either way, I was better. I was a good kid. These kids were a bunch of punks, a bunch of losers, a bunch of future nobodies. I'd go home after every session and tell my parents all about how I'd seen the light, how I was different from these druggies, how I had learned my lesson. No parent wants to believe their teenage kid is an alcoholic, so they fell for my antics.

Once they agreed to let me stop attending group therapy, and once some of the shame wore off, I took my summer-long grounding as an invitation to be better. I would clean up my act. I'd eat fewer carbs and calories. I'd lose more fat, build more muscle, and train harder than ever. I'd even read a few self-help books. I could sense perfection on the horizon, and a newfound hope lit my path. God was going to set me straight. I would finally live up to my potential. I was going to stop letting Him down.

Chapter 14

SOME SORT OF STUD

Following the White Water incident, the whole summer before junior year was dedicated to my aesthetic enhancement. Improving my body created a false sense of security, an ephemeral validation of my elusive okayness. The typical day consisted of a two-hour gym session, tennis practice, tanning by the pool, and the occasional summer reading. My need for speed started increasing. I was worn out. The diet pills warned me not to drink any additional caffeinated beverages. I didn't follow instructions and added chain-drinking Diet Coke to my regimen in order to keep up.

I became chummy with some of the older gym rats and personal trainers. They complimented my form and work ethic. The staff would give me free, quick tips if they ever saw an opportunity for improvement. Once, when I was running sprints on the treadmill after a lengthy weight-training session, the owner of the gym made an announcement to a group of his clients: "That's what dedication looks like, ladies and gentlemen. Nice work, Chris." I yearned for their approval.

My first deviation from the diet plan prescribed by *Be Fat Free Forever!* came in the form of an intervention. My tennis coach pulled me into his office after practice. He told me that I had lost enough weight, that I was dragging and needed more energy. We began discussing diets more tailored for athletes. I remember him telling me that all the world-class tennis pros ate the same thing every day. They treated their bodies like machines, and fueled them as such. I was afraid of adding carbohydrates back into my diet, but I reluctantly agreed to eat some before my workouts.

Not long after I reintroduced carbohydrates, a personal trainer at the gym gave me the tip to eat brown rice before bed in order to stimulate muscle growth. More carbs sounded scary, but added muscle growth was immensely appealing. Such was the conflict between skinny and muscular. I added this practice to my repertoire. Getting huge was ever so slightly more important to me than trimming down.

My dietary habits formed into a pristine eclecticism. I began reading as many diet books, men's magazines, and exercise strategies as I could get my hands on. I devised the perfect diet. Low-glycemic, high-protein, low-calorie, high-frequency, nutrient-dense meals became my religion. As I started gaining weight, I made sure that it was all lean muscle mass. If I ever gained any fat, I would just spend a couple of weeks restricting carbohydrates. Now standing at five feet, ten and a half inches, I got up to about 190 without going up in my body-fat percentage.

For the first time in my life, I was pleased with my body. To complete the makeover, I cut off my shaggy brown hair in exchange for a crew cut. Before long, I went full-blown narcissist, the sort of creepy shit you see in movies. I started masturbating in the mirror to myself. I found a spot in my room where there was overhead lighting, and I would flex in different poses after I worked out and had a nice pump. The stretch marks around my love handles and belly faded away. I started getting stretch marks around my shoulders, arms, and chest instead.

I bought new clothes. The old ones didn't fit. I got to wear the skinny brands now. For my school uniform, I picked out athletic-cut shirts that were tailored to taper down to the waist. I wore them one size too small to show off the guns. The first time I stepped foot back on campus at the end of summer, I was inundated with positive feedback. A few of the cheerleaders were there practicing, and one of them asked Alex, "Who is that hot guy you're with?" I was standing across the parking lot in my sleeveless shirt after a lifting session. Alex told me what she'd said, and I was floored. "Hot" was definitely not anything I had ever heard before. It made me blush.

The girls weren't the only ones who noticed. Guys in the gym, mostly football players, were shocked at my transformation. They wanted to know what I did. They asked me what I ate, what exercises, what supplements, everything. I became an instant expert in exercise and nutrition. Guys I had never even met before would approach me, asking questions like, "How do I get shoulders like yours?" One or two asked, "What are you on?" but I just humbly replied, "I drink a lot of protein powder." I had never really been athletic, and weight lifting became a way for me to get the high praise I'd never received as a child. It was a sport in and of itself.

I started finding ways to work out more. I'd wake up in the morning and do crunches and push-ups just to get my day started right. I began "engaging my core" all throughout the day, meaning I would flex my abdominal muscles around the clock. I read it was good for your posture and helped tone your abs. I'd refrain from using the backs of chairs in class, in order to strengthen my spine. I'd flex while I walked, creating a ridiculous strut effect. I didn't get teased anymore; if anything, I was flirted with. Guys would joke around about my muscularity, make fun of my protein intake at lunch, and remark that the only reason I wouldn't get stoned after school was because I had to hit the gym.

Now that my body was good enough, I was ready to fall in love again. There was a significant movement occurring at the time: the hookup culture. Going steady, being boyfriend and girlfriend, was just an option, whereas before it had been a necessity. If you were planning on getting lucky in late middle school and early high school, she needed to be your girlfriend, but not anymore. Hooking up was also something that went along with the weekend binge drinking. I'd get drunk and hope to have a handsy make-out session. Even though my bodily transformation made it fairly easy to hook up, my insecurity about my penis size and sexual performance did not.

Despite the whole hookup culture, I still found my target. Chloe was an athletic, doe-eyed brunette on the volleyball team, constantly a contender in the boys' ongoing debate over who was the hottest girl in school and, no joke, one of the coolest chicks in my class. She had it all. She was my unicorn, my great white buffalo, the solution to all of my problems.

Just as the script would mandate, we started out as friends. We didn't hook up. We just loved each other. We'd talk on the phone for hours. There was the time she told me she would die for me, and I was certain I'd do the same for her. My entire life quickly became an avenue for obtaining her affection. She was the one, and there was a rollover effect from all the other ones who'd come before. She inherited a great deal of transference.

It was torturous just being friends with her. I was too afraid to make a move, reserving any romantic disclosure for times when I was intoxicated, so I could blame my feelings on the alcohol in case she said no. The rejection would've been too much to handle. As a result, I became firmly entrenched in the friend zone, the dreaded area of no return, where testicles go to shrivel up and dreams go to die.

My friends started giving me a ton of shit about it. I was chastised for wasting my time on her and acting so "gay." I started hating her at times, and I would swear her off the way an addict swears off drugs. My friends even started joking that I was "using again" whenever I would hang out with her. They'd stick out their forearms and slap their skin, insinuating that I was back on the needle. I was. It got to the point that I even constantly tried to fall for someone else because the pain of such intense investment in a single person was overwhelming.

Whenever she would date another guy, I'd back off. I'd apply the tried-and-true methods of stonewalling her and acting supercold—the kind of stuff that worked in early adolescence—but it rarely had any impact except to hurt her feelings. I would even temporarily fall for other girls, but in the back of my mind, I knew I was reserving my true love for Chloe, waiting for the day that she could be mine.

Every sexual encounter, no matter how insignificant, was a way to validate my manhood in the face of such guarded vulnerability. There were times I would even drunkenly profess my love to Chloe, and then that same night, go hook up with girls I barely knew. Each empty conquest aimed to smooth the jagged terrain of my unlovable self. I was some sort of stud, a malignant mixture of testosterone and insecurity. God didn't like it one bit, but I blamed Him for His own faulty design.

Dry spells were the worst. I kept score, and if there were a few weeks that I didn't hook up with anyone, I'd desperately search for creative solutions. Next to our neighborhood Starbucks was a place called Spa of

Atlanta. We heard rumors that it was the kind of spot where you could get a "happy ending." A few of us were fascinated with the prospect of playing out our pornographic fantasies, so we gave it a try.

I cracked my mom's credit-card PIN, so I was able to withdraw funds whenever she loaned me her MasterCard for gas. Normally, we just used the cash for drugs and alcohol. When three of us pulled around the back of the lonely whitewashed building and got out of the car, we saw just one door with a floodlight shining on the entrance, a hot-pink neon OPEN sign, and one huge security camera only a foot or so away from us, pointing directly at our faces. Appropriately intoxicated, we rang the doorbell and tried to be cool for whoever was inside. A small old Asian lady wearing lots of makeup, a short colorful kimono, and clear, clunky high heels answered the door.

"IDs," she brusquely demanded.

I handed her my fake with what I thought was enough haste to meet her energy yet still come off as chill.

She glanced at the ID, looked me in the eye, and shouted, "You no twenty-one, you baby face!"

"Yes, I am," I rebuffed.

The bluff worked; she quickly granted me access to her secret sex lair.

Once inside, my friends and I were escorted down a long floral-print hallway. I was shown into a room on the left with a massage table in the middle and a walk-in shower in the corner, where I was told to undress and wait. A younger version of the boss lady, with the same colorful face, tiny kimono, and high heels, entered and began washing my body. I nearly ejaculated from the shower alone.

After bathing me, she had me lie down flat on the table, and within about ten minutes of erotic massage, she informed me of the price scale: "Hundred fifty sex, hundred blow job, fifty hand job."

"I'll take the hand job," I quavered, pretty sure this option gave me the best chance of avoiding an STD. I handed her three twenty-dollar bills: "Keep the change."

From then on, if I ever needed a quick release, a break from my Chloe-induced self-hatred, I knew where to go. It happened a handful of times, and I was always intoxicated, but I tried my best to refrain, since I was definitely sinning and my imaginary wife deserved better.

I half believed that if Chloe would just hook up with me here and there, I'd be able to move on, as if once the barrier had been broken, she'd cease to be such a dominating force in my bewildered psyche. At school, we were assigned free periods called study halls, but rather than study, the kids in those periods usually just hung out. I longed to be in Chloe's same study-hall period each trimester, and God answered my prayers. We ended up being in the same one for all of junior year. By the end of it, I was miserable. The more I hung out with her, the more I knew I was in love. She was all I wanted, and I couldn't have her. The most painful part was that I didn't even know how she felt. I was caught between anxiety and idolatry, as if Chloe weren't involved at all. The singular object of my every boyhood fantasy, she was driving me insane.

Chapter 15

TOTALED

In a matter of a few sober weeks, any recollection of my alcoholic tenden-
cies had long been forgotten: I buried my brief addiction counseling stint
deep in my subconscious. The first night my parents allowed me to sleep
over at a friend's house, I relapsed. I only sort of considered myself "alcoholic" at the age of sixteen, preferring to use the much-lamented label as
more of an adjective than a noun. I was paralyzed with anxiety in my first
social event since I'd been hospitalized for alcohol poisoning, and by this
time, I simply didn't know how to function at a party without drinking.
What would I say? What would I do with my hands? So I fell back on the
only solution I knew to work. I got drunk.

Mom and Dad kept catching me here and there, and they also kept
praying I would grow out of it. I nearly relished the weeks of restriction
accompanying each mishap, since my punishments allowed me more
space to diet and exercise. The social anxiety gained momentum with
every outing, and I was convinced that I couldn't have a social life without
drugs and alcohol. Each time I drank, I delayed the inevitable event where
I'd be forced to socialize without chemical aid. My intoxication was like a
double-edged sword, temporarily easing my anxiety and simultaneously
passing it on to my next sober engagement. Either way, I was damned.

Because my parents had gotten keen enough to test me when I got
home for curfew, I resorted to fairly extreme measures. The second I got

out of school on Friday, I would go to the park and chug one shot per hour that remained until curfew. If it was four o'clock, and I had to be home by eleven, I'd down seven measured shots of liquor as quickly as possible. I don't remember how I learned that one shot equaled one hour of metabolism, but it seemed to work just fine. With the help of copious amounts of marijuana and the occasional miscellaneous substance, I was good to go. I'd hit fast food a few minutes before checking in, just to be sure my breath didn't smell of anything other than a spicy chicken sandwich. Lastly, if that weren't enough, I would stealthily flip over the test strips as I placed them on my tongue.

The times I got grounded followed the evenings I was permitted to spend the night out. All I had to do was call my house by curfew from my friend's home line, so my parents could verify through caller ID that I was indeed where I'd said I would end up. So long as I could form coherent sentences, I passed. Despite the simplicity of these requirements to retain my privileges, I'd still fail. Without the guaranteed fate of alcohol strips and my mom's classic hug-to-smell tests, I'd struggle to remain conscious. I started blacking out regularly, yet even then, I'd still occasionally avoid disciplinary action, assuming I was able to straighten up and speak English for a couple of minutes.

When my folks went out of town, they'd leave Mimi and Poppy in charge. I was excited to plan a concert event during one of their stays, confident they wouldn't be required to carry out the routine. I was wrong. Poppy met me at the door upon my return, and with tears welling up in his eyes, meticulously read the testing instructions. He studied them so closely that he caught something my parents never did, that I needed to hold it on my tongue for at least thirty seconds. My only out was to perform my patented sleight-of-hand maneuver, the wrist-pivot strip flip. When I gave the test back to Poppy, he was confused. The test read negative, except for a frame-like outer edge, the color indicating extreme intoxication. The white area framed in black was suspect, but I assured him it was normal. What a victory.

There wasn't much a bunch of private-school Atlanta kids couldn't get away with back then. The public parks nestled away in the greater Atlanta suburbs were our stomping grounds. We'd go there after dark, often inviting girls to come with us but not always. Most of us knew the parks' terrain better than the cops, so it was actually great fun whenever we'd see their flashlights approaching. Our game was like a high-stakes version of capture the flag. We'd disperse and sometimes spend the entire evening excitedly inebriated, strategizing how to get back to our cars without getting caught.

Despite our regular shenanigans, the cops finally caught up to us. A bunch of us were at Chastain Park, in an area that wasn't as heavily wooded as the ones we usually grazed. We might have gotten away if we didn't think their headlights belonged to one of the girls. I went up to their car to greet them and was thoroughly shocked to see the men in blue. "Oh, hi, officers," I loudly proclaimed, hoping my friends would take the hint to ditch their goods.

They had us all line up in a row. I was hammered. There were about fifteen of us there, boys and girls. One of them took a flashlight to each of our faces, while the other one made a few announcements: "Public parks are closed after dark. If we catch you here again, we're going to take every one of you in." They walked around the premises, seizing a few cases of beer. "Listen up. We're going to let you guys off tonight, so long as we don't find any drugs." I wished I could feel relieved, but there was a bunch of weed in my truck.

One of the officers made his way to my car. There was a case of Bud Light on my passenger floor. "Whose truck is this?" he asked the group.

"It's mine, sir," I stoically replied.

"Is this your beer, son?" Trick question.

"Yessir," I said, hoping honesty would save the day.

The officer began searching in the backseat, near my secret stash. I thought I might have a heart attack. My buddy Frank took the opportunity to throw his little glass container of weed as far as possible while the officers were inspecting my car. It made a loud noise, since he was unable to avoid the distant sidewalk. We trembled in terror as the glass shattered on the pavement.

At the same time that the glass broke, the officers left my car. Some of the girls were crying. "Stay cool," we softly insisted. I was just glad they didn't find my contraband.

They stood in front of us again and began giving further instruction: "You're lucky we didn't find any drugs. I want you all to go home. If we see you here again after dark, we won't be so kind."

After each of us profusely thanked the officers, we rolled into our cars and slowly pulled away. I didn't stop freaking out until the next morning. They'd let me drive drunk away from the scene, so I feared they were tailing me, that maybe it was a trap. The sun came up without a hitch though; they didn't even call our parents.

My next encounter with the law didn't go so smoothly. Frank's girlfriend was having a birthday party, and I was going to spend the night out at his house afterward with my other friend, Greg. Naturally, I got slammed. Frank drove his own car, and when it was time to leave, Greg and I decided I was the most suitable choice to drive. It was raining, but I felt confident in my ability to brave the way. "I'm cool, just a little buzzed," I assured Greg, who was riding shotgun. I had to make curfew, so I was racing the clock. If I got to Frank's house late, my parents were going to ground me.

Frank lived about thirty minutes from his girlfriend, and I spent our whole drive staring at my car's digital timekeeper, gaining speed with each passing minute. I raced down the last major road of our route, rain beating against the windshield, accelerating into every turn. I began to fishtail out of control around a long stretch of road without a right-side shoulder. In my attempt to straighten out, I overcorrected, throwing us across the opposite lane. I was unable to avoid the lone car headed our way, forcing him to T-bone us on the passenger side, right where Greg was seated.

I'm lucky I didn't kill anyone that night. Greg was unharmed, saved by the enormous lift kit, the one I'd begged my dad to install on my Sport Trac in order to increase its off-road capabilities and general masculinity. When we got out, I hurled my case of beer in the direction of the nearby woods and approached the victim's car window. He was our age, probably just leaving a party himself. His little sedan looked totaled, the front entirely smashed in, but he said he was okay. My truck was obviously bent, but it didn't seem that bad since the impact had taken place underneath my vehicle's body.

The other driver started fretting about how he couldn't get another ticket, so I figured he'd been speeding. I told him not to worry, that my dad was a successful surgeon and could buy him a new car, so long as the cops didn't get involved. I hated that I was saying this, but it was the best reason my intoxicated mind could come up with to try to get him to keep the police out of it. We exchanged information, and I scribbled his name and number onto my forearm. I promised him that I'd call him in the morning and quickly pulled away.

Greg and I laughed hysterically, just thankful to be alive: "Holy shit, that was close!"

I parked my truck down the street from Frank's house and ran in to call my parents for curfew. All was fine enough; I'd worry about the wreck in the morning.

I lay down to go to sleep, but my heart was still pounding, and I was sick to my stomach, terrified of what my parents were going to think, what they might do to me. A few minutes later, the doorbell rang. It was the police. The officer asked, "Are you Chris Cole?"

"Yessir."

"Have you been drinking this evening?"

"Yessir."

"Was anyone else in your car?"

"Yessir."

He handcuffed me and Greg and escorted us into the back of his vehicle. As we pulled away, I saw my dad standing in the rain, examining my wrecked truck parked down the street. I guess he had already talked to the officer. I made eye contact with him as we passed. The police car's rainy window served as a mirror, revealing the son I had become. Still, I blamed my parents for all of it. If I hadn't been rushed to make curfew, I told myself, none of this would have happened.

I was booked for a misdemeanor—minor in possession of alcohol—and a felony, hit and run. The only way I avoided a DUI was that there was no proof of me drinking prior to the accident. When Dad bailed me out the next morning, his despair cut me to the core. The police shared with him the story of how I'd told the kid that my dad was loaded and would pay to keep him quiet. I found out our deal had fallen through when his car couldn't start. My former self, that little kid with the overactive moral compass, was nowhere to be found. Ideas of right and wrong were long gone, replaced with my theory of relativity, one that had me pegged squarely in the center of the universe.

Dad had never shared such hurtful feelings with me before. Disgusted, he tearfully confessed that he'd made mistakes by spoiling me. There was nothing worse than being called spoiled. I felt like the worst kind of kid imaginable, ungrateful for privilege and hell-bent on getting my way, no matter what the cost or whom I might hurt. In that moment of total disgrace, I could finally feel the impact. My dad worked his ass off to afford me every opportunity to thrive, and this was his reward.

We hired a high-priced lawyer to help me avoid any charges. He basically had me, in advance, do all the things that the judge would mandate in court. I spent endless hours volunteering at a local thrift store, logging the typical duration required of a first-time underage felon. I attended DUI classes, where I was shocked to learn that more than two drinks for an adult at any given time might indicate a drinking problem. I documented my attendance at ten Alcoholics Anonymous meetings, enduring a few and forging signatures for the rest. Finally, I wrote an essay outlining what I'd learned through the process and how sorry I was for my behavior.

On the day of my hearing, the lawyer advised me on standard etiquette in the courthouse and best practices in front of the judge. I wore a suit and tie, stood with my hands by my sides, and repeated, "Yes, your honor," until she pardoned me for my sins. She confirmed the formality: "Since you have already completed what the court would recommend for your case, you are free to go. All charges will be dropped."

Not so bad, I thought to myself. Pleasantly surprised to see how easy it was to buy my way out of trouble, I set out to hit the RESET button in hopes that my most delinquent behavior was already behind me.

My every intention called for a new and better existence, but after only a few weeks of remorse and sobriety, it was clear that nothing had really changed. The dial was cranked to addiction and disorder, so that no amount of intrapsychic discomfort led to sustainable action. I was stuck in perpetual anxiety and conflict, longing for sex but afraid of it, ashamed of my drinking but needing it, hating all my dieting and exercise rigidity but seeing my physique as the only solution to my lack of confidence and self-esteem.

Any moments of insight would be immediately repressed. I told myself that life would be different once I got to college. If I could only survive senior year, then I would be free. I rationalized the whole charade, blaming everyone but myself. *If I were allowed to drink, I wouldn't need to get drunk. If my parents weren't so strict, I wouldn't act so crazy.*

Chapter 16

CUT UP

The big lie, that my body was responsible for all my problems, was running out. I was in peak physical condition, but I was absolutely miserable much of the time. For my whole life, I'd thought that if I could just not be fat, everything would be perfect. No matter the size or shape of my body, going into senior year, I hated myself, and my body served as the proverbial punching bag for my every neurotic whim. I'd fixate on any flaws, hoping the biggest, strongest, leanest version of myself could rid me of the pain.

I couldn't keep up with what I had started. My diet began to slip. I was getting tired more quickly during workouts. I was constantly falling short of perfection. I began openly discussing my insecurities with my parents, relentlessly informing them of my shortcomings. Of particular concern was the presence of stretch marks, the remnants of my former fat self. I searched far and wide for remedies to combat these unsightly scars. I rubbed all sorts of lotions and oils on my belly to try to get rid of them, but even when they faded, it wasn't enough.

The stretch-mark complex was nothing compared to my nipple obsession. I was hyperfocused on my nipples' size and their protrusion through my shirt. In my mind, they were like puffy pepperoni patties large enough to require a bra. I was jealous of guys who had little skittle-sized nipples. I would make my nipples hard by rubbing on them with my forearms, to make them appear smaller. I slouched my shoulders forward to hide them. I started buying dark-colored and patterned shirts to obscure their visibility. I even wore my book bag backward for added protection.

When I wasn't ruminating over my stretch marks or nipples, I was fixated on my abs. My abdominal muscles represented my ultimate measure of worth, the standard of fitness and attractiveness. I read about the ideal body-fat percentage for washboard abs, and I was confused to find that I was in the range that typically allowed for the full display of one's six-pack. Despite my best efforts, I could only get the top four to pop.

My determination to get "cut" knew no limits. I even bought a topical solution at GNC that was supposed to melt away fat in the area it was applied. The product worked about as well as those penis-enlargement pills. It didn't take me long to realize that the reason my lower abdominal muscles were not showing was because I had loose skin from weight loss. "The pooch," as I called it when complaining to my parents, was a saggy area of skin right above my belt line. I hated it, and I convinced myself that it was the only difference between my body and Adonis-like perfection.

I started badgering my parents about my little tummy problem. I told them that my loose skin made me have a muffin top whenever I'd wear a bathing suit. I implored them to consider the pain of my dilemma, explaining how my pooch stuck out, insisting that girls could see it through my shirt. I made it sound as if my saggy belly and oversized nipples were the sole impediments preventing me from obtaining total peace of mind. I believed it.

Being the loving folks that they were, my parents wanted to help. They were hurting with me, and they would've done anything to take away my pain. Mom and Dad always had their own conflicts about balancing outer appearance with inner beauty. They collected diet books and stayed abreast of the latest health kicks, but so did the rest of America, and I didn't think much of it. They would tell me, "People say not to judge a book by its cover, but the reality is that they naturally do; that's why we have the saying in the first place, to remind us what's really important."

After I'd complained for long enough, they volunteered a new suggestion. They offered me a consultation with a local plastic surgeon, one who specialized in liposuction. My dad was a plastic surgeon after all, and although he only did face-lifts, he was still familiar with the various surgical solutions to body woes. I had minimal questions or concerns, and after a couple of conversations, I agreed to meet with the best lipo guy in Atlanta.

The whole deal was very secretive as I went to the doctor's office for my consultation. I didn't want anyone to know I was getting liposuction, so to get me out of school that day, we just said I was getting a checkup. Still, I was afraid someone was going to find out. Liposuction was about as extreme a measure as I could think of for enhancing my appearance. Even though I was fully entrapped by my own vanity, there was a voice of clarity crying out for me to wake up. As much I wanted to heed its advice, I couldn't see any other option.

In order to go through with it, I needed to get a mammogram. My nipple situation warranted an exam for breast tissue. A large black woman smushed my nipples into an enormous glass vise and took a few pictures. It turned out I had a minor case of gynecomastia, the presence of breast tissue in males, a benign condition but an embarrassing one nonetheless. My insanity was finally validated: "I really do have man boobs!" I considered that all of those testosterone boosters I was buying at GNC might have had something to do with it. The doc said he had seen much worse cases than mine and that it wasn't anything he couldn't fix in surgery.

I stripped down to my underwear for the surgeon, timidly awaiting his appraisal of my body. There were those fluorescent lights again. As I stood in the exam room with him and my mom, wearing nothing but my tighty-whities, the doctor took out a marker and circled all the fat around my stomach, back, and chest. I remember feeling like he was circling areas I hadn't even realized were a problem, something hard to do since I was so obsessive. *Man, I'm gonna be ripped*, I thought to myself.

I didn't feel any shame until he explained to me how the whole thing worked. I would go under anesthesia, so I wouldn't feel or remember the surgery. He'd make small incisions in my chest, back, and stomach, so he could reach the fat with a long tubular vacuum. The incisions would be barely noticeable, and he would strategically place them near moles and scars to minimize their visibility. The healing time would be a few weeks, during which I would wear a compression vest to make sure all the tissue adhered properly together. There would be bruising and discomfort but nothing I couldn't handle. His play-by-play made me uncomfortable, but I was already committed, so I just tried not to think about it.

My parents and I planned how we were going to keep it a secret, which added more feelings of shame, subtly affirming that I was doing something wrong. The surgery was scheduled for a couple of months before my eighteenth birthday, and since I was a minor, my parents had to consent to the operation. We scheduled the surgery over Christmas break, so I'd have some time to recuperate without missing school.

When I woke up from the anesthesia, my body ached. A large piece of paper was laid over me like a blanket. I lifted up the thin sheet to see bandages covering my torso. When I saw my body for the first time after the surgery, it looked like I'd been beaten with a baseball bat around my belly. What had I done? Had my body really been that bad? Was this going to make me feel better? I immediately regretted my decision, and I was mad at my parents, blaming them for encouraging me to do something I wasn't ready for, something I didn't understand. In my disillusionment, I felt that the doctor deserved to lose his license, that cosmetic surgery should be illegal for minors.

We told Tyler and Allison that I was sick, so they wouldn't suspect anything while I was bedridden. I used the same story with my friends. I didn't tell a soul.

I wasn't allowed to exercise while I recovered from surgery. I gained about ten pounds immediately, since I wasn't working out, so, ironically, my plastic surgery was interfering with my ability to maintain my physique. The prohibition on exercise left me despondent, and I was superparanoid about anyone finding out I'd had the procedure. I had to wear that damn compression vest under my school uniform, and I feared someone would feel it under my shirt. During gym class, I changed in the stalls, so no one could see my healing torso.

The surgery only served to increase my obsession and shame. I had to go to follow-up appointments, where I would get ultrasound treatments to help my tissue heal properly. The nurses put the clear jelly lube over my stomach as if I were a pregnant woman. I started asking the staff if it looked good, and if they thought it was complete. They assured me it looked great and that I was healed. I disagreed. I thought it looked fake—too smooth, obvious that a cosmetic procedure had taken place. I was angry with the results. My abs weren't popping enough, and I imagined that my abs showed even less after the surgery. I didn't believe my skin had healed correctly. There were a few times that I had gone to school without wearing my compression vest, and I considered that I might be to blame for the incomplete healing. My nipples were still too big and puffy. My waist was still festooned with tiny love handles. My parents tried to console me, insisting it looked right, but I didn't believe them. I didn't believe anybody.

I completely regretted the surgery. I was so ashamed. I hated that my parents had allowed me to go through with it. Vanity is one of the seven deadly sins, and I feared that my adolescent liposuction procedure would assure me a spot in hell. Not only that, but I thought it looked really strange and unnatural. I wished that I could make my belly go back to the way it was before. I wanted to be naturally attractive, not artificially enhanced.

Future predicaments played out in my mind. How could I tell my wife? What would she think of me? Getting liposuction felt like a weird and creepy thing to do, especially for a young man. I knew I'd have to keep it a secret for the rest of my life. Even then, my wife might notice the little scars and discover the truth, and then, since I'd lied about it, she would definitely leave me. What kind of psycho gets liposuction at seventeen? I was doomed.

Beneath the guilt and shame was some incredibly repressed aware- ness that it was impossible for me to be satisfied with my body. I started to recognize how sick I was, but I did my best to distract myself from this reality. The drug and alcohol abuse picked up, and even though I wanted to stop, I knew I couldn't. I imagined a day when I might be happy and content enough to carry on a normal conversation without needing to be inebriated. There was the person I longed to be somewhere deep within, but he was unable to get out. The soul God had thrown into this life, the one destined for greatness—he was lost with little hope of return.

Part Two

EXODUS

Chapter 17

HAZED AND CONFUSED

A big ego with little identity, I set out for the promised land. College was going to fix everything. I couldn't wait to get out from under my parents' supervision, and by the time I turned eighteen, they were worn out, ready to let me either sink or swim on my own.

Jason and I left early for the University of Georgia, before Henry and Chloe and the rest of the incoming freshmen. We enrolled in a three-hour summer-semester course of microeconomics, moved into the dormitory, and began shopping our services to the various fraternities, hoping to fully matriculate from high school adolescence to collegiate manhood. As far as I could tell, college was just one big party, so at first, I was in heaven.

Fraternity life had more rules than I could digest, but so long as I stayed drunk and high, they didn't seem to bother me much. Homophobia reigned, racial slurs earned extra credit, and the more you made the guys laugh about your recent sexual exploits, the better. It took me only a few weeks to turn into a complete asshole. I was just following the rules.

To complicate matters, my penis betrayed me again. I ended up getting drunk and losing my virginity to my childhood friend Ashley; only I wasn't sure if I had technically lost my virginity or not because I didn't climax. We did it after a long night at the bars, in the dark, on the cold floor of this little pantry room in my dormitory where everyone microwaved their food. I told her I didn't have a condom, to which she replied, "Ever heard of pulling out?" and that was that. My first time was a wreck, and I was so nervous and drunk that I lost my erection. When I saw her a few days later, she whispered in my ear, "I know your secret," and I couldn't figure out if she meant that I had a small dick, that I couldn't finish, or that she had my v-card, but regardless, I was mortified. The remaining fragments of my imagined integrity were disintegrating fast, but I just channeled all my neuroses into finding the right fraternity.

My obsessive mission to join the best frat in Athens appeared to be running smoothly until I blacked out and began talking to a bunch of brothers about my inevitable bid to join Sigma Chi. They didn't like my presumptuous attitude. Gaining access to their secret club was considered a great privilege, not an entitlement to be tossed about in such a cavalier fashion. Jason gave me a pep talk, encouraging me the next day to tone it down. Even though I tried to take the whole discussion in stride, the mere prospect of rejection, the chance that they might not welcome me into their group, put me on guard.

Jason and I headed up to Hilton Head for Sigma Chi's annual beach weekend, where it was rumored a large number of incoming freshmen would receive bids. Everyone was excited, but I was still feeling embarrassed about my belligerent faux pas of a few days before. The brothers doled out my punishment as I watched every invited freshman receive a bid except for me. My peers were snuck into a private room and showered with beer and congratulations all night, as if they'd won the World Series. I tried not to sulk, attempting to drink away familiar feelings of envy and alienation. I cried my eyes out when we got back to the hotel room, chain-smoking cigarettes and attempting to rationalize my rejection. The next day, there was a strange silence between me and Jason on our ride home, where he tried to contain his excitement while I pretended nothing had happened.

The following weekend, I accepted my bid from another fraternity, Pi Kappa Phi, at their respective beach event. It felt nice to belong, especially given my recent rejection, but I was sad that I wouldn't be in the same fraternity as my best friend. When I got back, Jason was annoyed with me. I didn't need to accept the bid, he said. I could have easily held out.

He was right: the Sigma Chi brothers soon invited me to another of their parties without knowing I had already pledged somewhere else. I tried my best to block out the thought that I'd made a catastrophic mistake. I had to stay strong, since I'd already made my decision. Then Henry came up one weekend and accepted a bid to Sigma Chi as well, so just like that, I was separated from my two childhood friends, the only two guys in Athens who knew me before I turned into such a bewildered buffoon.

After a couple more weeks of barhopping and house parties, fall semester finally arrived. Many of my peers had already accepted bids, but we still went through the formality of rush week, during which incoming freshmen toured all of the fraternities and received invitations to parties, where the last of the remaining bids would be handed out. I hung out at the frat house all day and served as an extension of the rush committee, welcoming my peers and telling them why Pi Kappa Phi was the place to be.

There was one black freshman, dressed in preppy clothes, touring the house with the rest of the rush crowd. A few of the brothers made jokes: "Is he lost? Chris, go tell him where he can find the black fraternities." In that moment, I realized what should have been obvious from some of the brothers' incessant racism and Confederate flag décor: black people weren't allowed in this fraternity. I had successfully reached a new low.

When I saw a few of my high-school friends touring the house, I begged the brothers to give them bids. I seriously needed some familiar faces in my new family. I briefly considered going back to Sigma Chi, with my tail between my legs, to ask for another chance, but it would have been too embarrassing, and there was no guarantee they'd still have me. I had to just stick it out. So much secret pain brewed, and even with an endless supply of chemical aids, I could barely keep the lid on. The distress of pledgeship consumed my entire consciousness.

I'd spent my whole summer semester partying with these guys, but now, all the Pi Kappa Phi brothers began telling me about how I was going to get it the worst during hazing. It was probably all in good fun, because I really did believe they liked me, but I started getting paranoid. I imagined what their threats meant, and visions of them forcing me to get naked in front of the whole fraternity were humiliating, even in the privacy of my own mind. I could see them pulling down my pants and spanking me with paddles. I tried to play it cool, but no amount of beer could fully silence my fears.

Pi Kappa Phi held a meeting prior to our first band party of the semester, in which my fellow pledgebrothers and I were given a dress code and general guidelines for pledgeship. We weren't allowed to wear sandals. We had to wear a tucked-in, collared shirt at all times. If we wore shorts, they had to stop clearly above the tops of our knees. We couldn't wear jeans, jewelry, or hats. My puka-shell necklace and confirmation ring had to go, and I went to the mall to buy some shorter shorts. We couldn't have any facial hair, but, as I was unable to grow a beard, that was fine by me.

The brothers gave us strict orders to be at the Pi Kappa Phi house before our band party that night. Even though I missed Jason and Henry, it felt good to be making friends with my newfound pledgebrothers, and the presence of a few of my high-school buddies eased the transition. When we arrived, dressed neatly in our frat uniforms, they had us all squeeze into one of the bedrooms, where we anxiously awaited further instruction. The air-conditioning was turned off, so the twenty or so of us stood around sweating, speculating as to what was about to happen in our first hazing experience.

A brother tossed in a case of warm beer and announced, "You guys can't come downstairs to the party until you finish this case." I was relieved. Drinking beer, even if it was hot beer, didn't seem like hazing to me. I chugged a couple of them to be a team player, and within a few minutes, we reported that we'd finished the job. Right when we thought we were out of the woods, another case arrived with the same instructions. "Oh shit," we collectively sighed, trying to guess how much warm beer we'd have to consume in this tiny sweatbox.

I decided to take on a leadership role with my new cohort and downed as many cans as I could. The beers kept arriving, and I kept on chugging. Before I knew it, I was vomiting all over the little bathroom. The loud moans of my pledgebrothers informed the leaders of the exercise that I'd had enough. One of them escorted me out of the room, and that's the last thing I remember.

I woke up a few hours later, hugging a toilet. When I went downstairs, the party was over and nearly everyone was gone. I called around and met the guys downtown at one of the bars. It wasn't my first puke-and-rally.

The brothers reamed me for being such a lightweight. One of the friendlier brothers asked, "Why didn't you just pour the beer down the sink?" I guess I never thought about trying to beat the system. I just wanted to be the best pledge I could be.

Even though I was always blaming my folks for my behavior, I missed the safety of their home and my little high-school existence. College life wasn't turning out at all as I had imagined it would. Now that I had spent the entire summer blacking out and embarrassing myself without my parents' supervision, it was fast becoming clear that I was the problem, and not them. Their disciplinary actions were probably the only reason I hadn't already destroyed my life. Now, Jason and Henry were the closest people I had to family, and since we were pledging different fraternities, I felt like we weren't even allowed to be friends.

Mom and Dad came up to Athens to help me move into my new dorm room, and I remember them saying how sick and pale I looked. My body was aching, I got really sweaty anytime I was sober, and my hands were starting to shake. They both cried when they reluctantly left me to go back home. Later, I wondered what would have happened if they had just taken me home right then, if maybe they could have saved me from what was coming. But the truth was, no one could save me—because I was absolutely unwilling to get honest, totally refusing to ask for any help.

Chapter 18

THE BIG BANG

In just the couple of months since I'd gone off to college, sanity had become a luxury. The various layers of ego converged to create a psychic density worthy of my own little big bang. I had no choice but to explode. My last few weeks before the explosion were a catastrophic crescendo of psychological upheaval. These days sent me swirling in my own confusion and shattered whatever weak identity remained. Full-blown insanity was my inevitable reality.

The week prior to fall semester's commencement was full of partying, and per usual, I found a way to get blackout drunk. I woke up in one of Chloe's friends' apartments to find permanent marker all over my thighs. There were arrows drawn to my crotch, and the words *small dick* and *tiny penis* were written in girls' handwriting. These were girls I had known since high school, and in that moment of regained consciousness, I wished for God to go ahead and kill me off.

As with many of my blackouts before, I wanted to know what had happened but was too afraid to ask. Had one of them hooked up with me? Had I taken my shorts off? Had I said something about my dick to them? Drawing on drunk, passed-out people was no new phenomenon; however, the possibility that they'd just thought of something funny to write on my legs never occurred to me. I assumed the worst. They had found me out.

Jason had been with me the night before, so I called him to pick me up. When I sat down in his passenger seat, my shorts slid up my thighs, revealing the markings.

"What happened there?" he laughed, but I just played it off. I didn't even ask Jason if he knew what had happened. I didn't want to know.

I started thinking incessantly about the ramifications of what had occurred. I imagined the girls telling all of their friends and sorority sisters that I had a little dick. I could see rumors that I was hung like a newborn infant spreading rapidly across campus. I would never get a girlfriend, let alone Chloe.

As if my chances to win over Chloe's affection weren't slim enough, she immediately started dating an older guy once she got up to Athens. I was devastated. I thought things would be different now that we were in college. I was going to show her I was no longer a high-school boy, that I was now a college man. I didn't want to be her friend; I wanted to be her lover. This was never going to change, and she needed to understand. On top of it all, I heard her new boyfriend was a total player. It wasn't fair. She deserved more, someone like me.

Even though a considerable amount of mental energy was being spent on Chloe's affairs, I had more pressing concerns to deal with regarding the fraternity. I was growing increasingly frightened of the prospect of hazing. I kept hearing all sorts of rumors of emotional and physical abuse. Older fraternity brothers, who were previously buying me shots, were now telling me that they'd soon be coming to collect, that they were going to make my life a living hell. Nothing much besides threats and rumors had occurred, but I was getting extremely anxious about what was coming.

My pledge class decided to throw a kegger at one of the guys' apartments downtown, and I began inflating it into this huge event, imagining that I alone was in charge of the party's success. Pale and sweaty, with trembling hands, I called everyone I knew that afternoon to share my excitement about what would be the greatest party of all time, but hardly any of my friends showed up.

A nervous wreck, I began suspecting that I had already turned into a real alcoholic. I asked an older fraternity brother about my hands shaking, and he encouraged me just to take a few days off drinking, saying that it would go away. "I'll stop drinking on Sunday," I told him as I cracked open my first beer of the weekend.

I found out during the party that a brother in another fraternity, a close friend of some of my older buddies, had died in a boating accident earlier that day. His tragic death ripped open a wound I'd never given a chance to heal. Seeing so many guys upset about their friend dying stirred up buried emotions about Sam and Isaac, as well as the general existential anxiety about my uncertain yet inevitable death. I didn't even know the kid; I didn't need to. It was all the same to me: another young man taken away from his family and friends, another story reminding me that life ends suddenly and without warning.

Over the next few hours, I grew increasingly fixated on this stranger's death, and I got more upset each time I heard someone talking about him. I began crying uncontrollably. People just assumed that I knew him really well. They comforted me in my grief. It was suggested that I drink up to deal with the hurt, and so I did. For the first time in my life, though, I was unable to get drunk. I couldn't ease my anxiety no matter how much alcohol I consumed.

That night, I watched the sun come up, all the while hoping to achieve some level of relief that never came. When I finally decided to crash on my pledgebrother's couch for some much-needed rest, I couldn't sleep. I felt like I was going to jump out of my skin. My entire body felt restless, and my mind was spinning about a hundred miles an hour. I probably didn't lie there for more than five minutes before I was out the door. I set out on foot, with about a half mile to get back to my dorm room.

It felt good to walk. I couldn't stop moving, so I might as well get some exercise. On my way home, I began to have another crying spell. I didn't even have words to put to the emotion. It was soul sadness, so deep it felt like it was coming from God Himself. I searched my mind for any logical reason that might help me understand such profound grief, but I was at a loss. My sorrow seemed without origin.

I ran into campus police while weeping through one of the parking lots on the way back to my room. I wished to avoid them, but we were the only two parties in the otherwise vacant lot. They stopped me to ask how I was doing. I told them that I was grieving my friend who'd died in a boating accident. They didn't ask me any further questions and suggested that I go find someone to lean on.

I took their advice and went over to Jason's apartment instead of back to the dorms. I knocked on the door, waking him up around seven o'clock. We sat down in his living room as I attempted to catch him up on the urgency of my situation. I told him how I couldn't stop crying, that I'd been crying since yesterday. He suggested that I go home for the weekend and see my parents, but there was no way I could face them in such a condition. They might never let me come back.

We ended up grabbing breakfast at Waffle House, and I started feeling better once I got some food in my system. Over the course of the meal, my spirits were lifted. I felt fabulous even. I started making grandiose comments about how I might study political science and try to be the next president of the United States. "We can do anything we want, be anything, go anywhere!" I was in total awe of the endless possibilities that lay before us as college freshmen. I wasn't crying anymore, so Jason dropped me off at my dorm to get some sleep.

Walking up the sidewalk to the dormitory, as God would have it, I ran into Chloe. Any idea of going to sleep disappeared immediately. A rush of the warm fuzzies came over my body, nearing orgasmic proportions. I missed her. She was getting in her car to run errands, so I asked if I could tag along. I would do anything to spend time with her. Being in her presence had a way of making me forget about everything else in the world.

It didn't take Chloe long to figure out something was strange with me. My speech was rapid and forceful. The need to catch her up on my life was powerful and overwhelming. When I started talking about pledgeship, she could tell the prospect of hazing was freaking me out. She encouraged me to talk to her brother, who was a senior in the same fraternity. I agreed to get on the phone with him.

During the call, I began to lose touch with reality. He was telling me that everything was going to be okay, that everyone goes through it and nothing crazy happens. "It's all part of the process," he assured me. "It's normal to feel how you're feeling." My mind suddenly loosened and became extraordinarily spacious, as a sense of serenity exploded in my consciousness. My interpretation of his emotional validation was that I was somehow experiencing special superhuman powers, part of being initiated into the fraternity's secret society. My whole body flooded with joy. I hung up.

Chloe asked me what he'd said. With a huge, intractable smile, I reported, "I can't tell you. It's a fraternity secret."

She quickly grew frustrated with my antics, but I didn't care; I suddenly had new priorities. I asked her to drop me off at the fraternity house, so I could fill the brothers in on the good news of my spiritual awakening. Once there, I ran upstairs to share my elation about my newly discovered psychic abilities and entered the first room with an open door. One brother was there, cleaning his room, and I just kept winking at him, thinking he could read my mind. He probably assumed I was high on drugs. He laughed and told me to go find my pledgebrothers: "Those guys are your brothers now. I don't want anything to do with you."

Feeling like a little kid again, before there was any pain or responsibility, I headed toward the dorms for the third time. It was a beautiful sunny day, and I began to feel as if I'd never set eyes on the world before now. In a flash, every sight and sound seemed so magnificent, and I felt delicate and light, as if transformed into an angel. I ripped my shirt off to feel closer to the sun's warmth. I'd never been so high, and I only briefly considered what could have landed me in such an altered reality. It felt kind of like I was on mushrooms, kind of like marijuana, and kind of like a combination between Adderall and ecstasy, but definitely something all its own. Alert and elated, I was overflowing with euphoria. I'd discovered heaven on earth, and to my recollection, I hadn't taken anything.

I was waking up from this bad dream named "Chris Cole," and my new identity was beyond my body, beyond my mind. I could only feel my soul. I saw that all of life was just an illusion, a game devised by my highest consciousness, by God. "Life is just a dream!" I wanted to shout it from the mountaintops.

I ran into a Sigma Chi brother at the bus stop. Fully convinced I'd imagined my entire life and ecstatic over the sudden realization of my spiritual existence, I told him how relieved I was not to have a dick the size of an acorn. He laughed awkwardly, like maybe I was talking crazy as a joke. I literally believed I was someone else, something superhuman, that this body, this life, wasn't actually mine.

As fast as my identity disappeared, I grasped for something new, some solid ground to stand on, any reference point to keep me from bursting into light. Colors looked more vibrant. Even the air smelled fragrant, like I was picking up the faint perfume of distant flowers. A wave of utter bliss permeated every fiber of my being.

Then my mind came back online, struggling to connect the dots: "This is what God feels like; I must be Jesus!" I knew I was sober, so I concluded that I must be the Second Coming of Christ. Time to tell the world. Everyone would be thrilled to hear the good news. The Son of Man had finally arrived! Peace on earth and love for all!

I ran upstairs to find my pledgebrothers, since I figured they would be my first disciples. When I got to my floor, they were all wide-eyed and happy to see me, but once I started incoherently rambling about my realized divinity, all they could do was aggressively ask, "Dude, what the hell are you on?"

I couldn't understand why they were so slow on the uptake. I pleaded with God to let me perform some miracles for them. I closed my eyes tightly and tried to concentrate; maybe God would make me fly or turn me into an animal, but my inability to levitate led to paranoia, and the thought that I had unknowingly been given drugs began to frighten me. Had someone spiked my drink the night before with LSD? I immediately started having a panic attack. My chest got tight. I couldn't breathe, and it felt as if my heart would stop beating or possibly explode. *I'm dying!*

They implored me to lie down on the futon in my dorm room, and a few of them tried to restrain me. The room, small to begin with, felt to me like a tiny box where I would soon suffocate to death. The army of pledgebrothers did their best to calm me down, but the longer they held me there, the more terrified I became. I shook them off my body, stood up, and punched one of them in the face, yelling, "You're the devil!" I then ran downstairs, desperate to break free of Satan and his minions.

When I made my way to the lobby, Jason was entering the building. One of my pledgebrothers had called him, and he was concerned. Seeing his face relaxed my whole body. I suddenly felt safe. He encouraged me to sit down with him on a nearby couch, where I proceeded to explain what was happening to me. I started loudly prophesying about healing the world with math, and began telling everyone in my proximity what his or her role would be in the new earth. I had no idea how I was coming up with this stuff; it was pouring out of me, as if from a channeled source.

Before I knew it, those same two campus police officers, the ones who had stopped me in the parking lot early that morning, entered the lobby. I lay down on the ground and put my hands behind my back. I knew they had come for me. In front of all my peers, I was handcuffed and escorted out of the building, but I felt calm, like it was all part of God's plan. When I got into the back of the car, they looked at each other, presumably a little shocked at my compliance, and one of them asked, "What should we do with him?" After a long sigh, the other replied, "Let's just take him in."

On my way to jail, I figured out that the cops were the Pharisees, and they were taking me to get crucified, so my short-lived tranquility instantly vanished. *This isn't how it's supposed to go*, I thought. *I just found out; I need more time!* I started pleading with God to spare my life, promising I'd do whatever He needed me to, that I'd had no idea what kind of big plans He had in store for me until today. I prayed and prayed, begging for forgiveness, hoping He might save me from their torture.

I was placed in my own cell, the special one reserved for the violent or psychotic. Locked inside, I completely fused with my delusions. No separation remained, and what followed was a series of events that, when recalled, seem to have felt like an out-of-body experience, in which I was watching a movie of myself with little to no control of the actor.

I stripped off all my clothes and started pacing in circles, running my fingers along the bumpy, painted concrete of the cell walls, as if I'd never experienced texture prior to now. I soon began shouting through the glass divide, insisting that the police officers come look at my penis. I needed them to see how small it was, to prove I was not of this world, to show them I was neither man nor woman.

A few of the officers joked, "Go look, maybe it will shut him up." The lucky officer encouraged to bear witness to my nakedness came over to the window, looked down at my crotch, shrugged his shoulders, and said back to the others, "Yeah, it's pretty small." They all laughed. I knew right then, confined to that holding cell, that God had given me this body to test my faith, to see if I truly trusted in His holy plan.

I was so anxious, restless, and jittery that I had to keep moving, pacing and drumming my fingers against the walls. I felt like every cell of my body was on high vibration, as if I might burst into flames. I was performing Morse code, communicating to the angels of heaven that I was ready for them to come rescue me. Instead, a number of officers started gathering near my cell door. Terror took hold: *Holy shit, they're going to crucify me!* A female officer showed me a gun and told me that if I resisted, she would shoot me with it. I pleaded with the gang of Pharisees for my life. "Don't shoot," I cried out, "don't shoot!"

The group of officers had me climb into a restraining chair, strapped down my body, handcuffed me, and chained my arms to the seat. An old man in a white lab coat came walking out of a back room, holding a large syringe. He pointed it in the air, and squeezed out a small stream of fluid.

Oh God, lethal injection. Please, God, no!

He sat down next to me.

"Please don't kill me!" I begged. "I'm sorry! I'm so sorry!"

Chapter 19

BORN AGAIN

I woke up in the same place they'd killed me, only now I had on some underwear.

I scanned the room to make sure I was indeed alive. A young woman walked slowly across the window and peered into my cell. She was crying, and though it was probably because she had recently been arrested, I imagined her tears were for me. I searched for an authoritative presence, but the girl seemed all alone. When she exited my view, I started to scream, "Help! Someone help!"

I was back in reality, but it all felt surreal, as if my dream and waking lives had permanently merged into one. I lifted my arm to the clanking of chains. I continued to scream: "Someone get me out of here!" I made as much noise as I could, rhythmically clanking the chains against my seat and crying for assistance. A few minutes later, an officer came to the window. "Pipe down. Someone will be with you shortly."

I must have been unconscious for several hours, because my parents showed up to bail me out a few minutes later. If I had known my folks were coming, I might have elected to stay in chains. They had a defeated look on their faces. Dad looked angry, and Mom had been crying. The officers explained to us that they had the whole ordeal on video, but it would remain confidential so long as the footage wasn't required in court.

The prevailing assumption was that I had taken drugs. It was dark out when we got into my parents' car to drive home to Atlanta. I started explaining to them what had happened, that I was the Second Coming, but they were dumbfounded, trying to understand what was happening to me, what might have occurred at school, and to what degree their son was presently coherent.

I felt like a caterpillar transformed into a butterfly. When we got back to the house, I took off my clothes and declared I was delivering humanity back to the Garden of Eden, that I was living the way God had originally intended. I explained to my parents that they were the reincarnation of Mary and Joseph, then went on to try to convince them of my immaculate conception, explaining that God had intercepted my father's seed. I had come to make good on my promise of heaven on earth. My whole life I had wondered why I was so different, so alone; everything finally made sense.

My dad took out the video camera, thinking it would be a good idea to document my behavior in order to show me later what I looked like on drugs. I welcomed the documentary and imagined this would be important proof for all the news outlets. I couldn't think of a better way to show the world that Jesus had arrived than to catch it on camera. In my mind, CNN would soon be informed of my descent, and I'd be giving speeches on Capitol Hill, broadcast across the globe. The world would rejoice in my long-awaited return.

My parents hoped that whatever drugs I'd consumed would wear off overnight, but the next morning, I was still gone. I dressed up in costumes. Each color I put on signified my royalty. I adorned myself with every piece of jewelry I could find, and clung tightly to my rosary. I carried my Bible around like some sort of magical shield.

I would open scripture to random pages, and each passage proved to validate my delusions that I was the same as Jesus. No matter what page I turned to, I would find spiritual truths regarding my life and inevitable arrival on Earth. I landed on John 1:12–13: "Yet to all who did receive him, to those who believed in his name, he gave the right to become children of God—children born not of natural descent, nor of human decision or a husband's will, but born of God." The only thing I was certain of was that

God had sent me to save humanity. I searched the Bible for secret clues, anything that might inform me of what needed to happen next.

Since God had blessed me with another beautiful sunny day, it was hard to stay indoors. I exited to the backyard, believing nature might transfer her healing powers to me. I was compelled to roll gleefully around in the grass, and our dogs ran in circles around me, excited to welcome me back to Earth. It was apparent that the animals recognized my sanctity. My dogs knew the truth, that God had sent His son to save the world, but my family still needed some convincing. The animals weren't inhibited by human intellect. Mom and Dad were anxious, fearing for my sanity, calling various professionals to figure out what to do with me.

My brother and sister were still in high school, and they were equally freaked out. I invited Tyler to join me in the hot tub, since I needed to be baptized again, and Mom asked him to keep watch while she ran some errands. As I dunked myself in the water, my body felt renewed. I continued to submerge myself and discovered that I could hold my breath for extraordinary lengths of time. Tyler panicked and reached into the water to save me. When I came up, I realized how much I was scaring him, but it didn't matter to me. He thought I might drown myself, but he didn't know my secret: I was not of this world, and God wouldn't let me die.

I started asking God to go ahead and give me some special powers, since clearly my sublime awareness and comprehension of scripture were not enough to convince my family of His plans. When we got back inside the house, I grabbed one of our pool cues and called it my staff. Moses needed a staff to perform his miracles, so I thought I'd give it a try. When I couldn't do any magic, I decided that God didn't want me to perform miracles this time around. This trip to Earth would be so I could teach people how to live on the real, within the parameters of their humanity. I needed to show them God's love without any magic tricks.

I begged my parents to take me to see a priest, so I could share the good news with someone who understood matters of the divine. At the very least, a priest could perform an exorcism, since I was starting to fear that maybe the devil was trying to get to me. After some convincing, my dad agreed to arrange a visit with one of our clergymen. I was having revelations, just like our biblical characters, so surely a priest would understand. When we got to our neighborhood church, the priest had my dad and me come to the altar. I figured we would talk for a while, so I could confer on him God's wishes, but all he did was ask me if I believed in the virgin birth. I paused for a moment and confessed, "No."

Upon my incorrect answer, he performed the sacrament—"anointing of the sick." He blessed me, and rubbed oil on my forehead. I was unimpressed. I'd thought that if anyone was going to understand, it would have been a priest. In that moment, I concluded God and I were once again in this alone. I could see that not a lot had changed since the last time we gave this a go. *"Forgive them, Father, for they know not what they do."*

The more I tried to figure out what was happening, the more I realized humanity's misunderstanding of my original teachings. My commandment was to love, and that was all that mattered. These humans, caught up in miraculous mythology, were missing the point. If I'd known walking on water would cause so much confusion, I wouldn't have done it. I doubted whether I'd ever performed any miracles in the first place. Miracles were for fairy tales. The real magic was unconditional love for all of God's children. I was ready to impart this truth to the world. There would be no more suffering, no more war, no more death. The time for peace on earth was now, and I had come to deliver us from evil.

The secret hurt of my life had risen to the surface, revealing the perfect delusion, the solution to all my neuroses. There couldn't have been a more isolated or perfect figure than Jesus, God's sole descendant, the singular avatar able to save humanity from its history of suffering, the only one who could make all this pain go away. Ever since I could remember, I had been alienated from every person I ever loved, had forbidden them from entering the truth of my vulnerable, aching heart.

I had to be Jesus, or else I couldn't go on; the pain was simply too much to bear.

Chapter 20

OVER THE RAINBOW

My parents scheduled an intake assessment for me at Ridgeview Institute, the acute psychiatric facility right outside of Atlanta. When they let me know I was going to the hospital, I replied, "Great, they can prove I'm God." I envisioned the doctors studying my blood under microscopes, astonished to discover some never-before-seen cellular activity that would confirm my divinity. They'd report their findings to the government, and before long, the CIA would place me under top-secret protection. President Bush would consult me, and I would soon counsel the United Nations toward peace on earth and love for all.

When we got to the hospital, I noticed that Ridgeview's logo included a rainbow, which pleased me greatly. In a flash of insight, I was awestruck by the magnificent simplicity of God's personalized sign for me. *This must be how Moses felt when he saw the burning bush*, I thought. The rainbow came after the storm. It was all so beautiful, so poetic, so enchanting. I could feel the synchronicity of God's every movement. I had cracked the code. I had weathered the storm, and now I could see: *I am the light signifying the end of humanity's suffering.*

Dr. Simpson, the psychiatrist on call, was an older man with a friendly smile. During our conversation, he plainly asked me, "What do you think is happening here, Chris?" Excited to transmit my vast and sudden knowledge of God's mysteries, I informed him that my wisdom would be easier to explain if he gave me a sheet of paper to draw on, that my truth was beyond words. When he pulled out a loose piece of printing paper, I frantically drew an image of the sun, placed my right hand over it, and proceeded to gyrate my body excessively in order to show him how the source of all life was now flowing through me.

The kind doctor nodded and smiled at my theatrical display, informing me that I needed to stay for further evaluation. After I'd said goodbye to my crying parents, a young, clean-cut, redheaded nurse walked me down a maze of hallways until we came upon a few zombie-like characters eerily pacing a large, open area.

He asked me to describe in my own words what was going on.

"I'm Jesus," I told him.

He replied, "Where's your white horse? Jesus comes again riding a white horse."

The priest hadn't believed me either. I found myself in a sad quandary: God didn't want me to perform any miracles, but if I didn't, no one was going to listen.

The psych ward felt oddly familiar, a cross between a motel and an emergency room, with white walls, bright lighting, and cheap furniture. I had a schizophrenic roommate, but I didn't know anything about mental illness, so he just seemed quirky to me. I asked him why he was there, and he told me this long, bizarre story about refusing to take his medication. He asked me the reason for my stay, and I told him, making a point to let him know that nobody believed me. He said, "How do *they* know you're not Jesus?" My thoughts exactly; I liked this guy.

The next couple of days were spent prophesying heaven on earth, chain-smoking cigarettes, and performing strange rituals with the hospital snacks. I learned the joy of smoking filterless menthols. I would count the number of various food items and try to decipher their biblical connotations. Three graham crackers plus two Jell-Os directed me to chapter five of whichever book I randomly opened to. I'd write furiously in my notepad, documenting all the rules for God's new world order. I was especially fixated on detailing the uniforms that I foresaw would be necessary, an odd perversion of the Pi Kappa Phi pledge dress code. I'd pretend the medicine line was for some sort of communion. I'd retreat to my little room, where I'd shower and masturbate and talk to God in the mirror. I'd come out naked, flashing my fellow patients, declaring, "We've returned to Eden. This is heaven. Welcome home!"

I made some nice friends. One girl told me she was a Playboy Bunny, and without being rude, I tried to figure out why she didn't look the part. She had a fresh tattoo across her back, some inspirational song lyric coded in Latin. I could tell she was crazy, since she clearly wasn't hot enough to be in *Playboy*. Another lady thought she was the Mother Mary, but I already knew my mom was the blessed virgin, so she was obviously insane. The woman was so happy to be reunited with me that she cried tears of joy, so I didn't have the heart to tell her the truth.

I discovered the phone and started calling Chloe to inform her of God's great plans for us. I had to tell her how she was the reincarnation of Mary Magdalene. God had sent us back to Earth so we could be together again, only this time we could get married and have sex. It all felt exceptionally romantic to me, so I was certain she would be breaking up with her boyfriend and looking forward to my return. When I got out, we would spearhead God's new religion together. She soon stopped answering the phone. I was scaring her.

Despite my exuberant high, these blissful delusions were punctuated with moments of horrible irritability and paranoia. The devil was trying to kill me, and I suspected that many of his soldiers were also staying in the hospital. I began doubting my delusions, and the thought that I might instead be the reincarnation of Lucifer crept into my consciousness. Maybe I wasn't in heaven, I fretted. Maybe this was hell. I was either all good or all bad, and I couldn't decide which one.

I quickly grew hostile. The hospital looked like it was swarming with demons, and many of the patients and staff members appeared ghoulish and sinister.

"I don't belong here! I'm Jesus fucking Christ! Call the president!" I picked up a chair and threatened to fight my way out of the building. Immediately, two huge staff members wrestled me to the ground and carried me, kicking and screaming, into a small padded room. Another man entered with one of those syringes again. They pulled my pants down and injected me in the ass. I woke up alone, and after I yelled for help, one of the staff appeared, telling me that I could come out once I was quiet for ten minutes straight. It took forever.

The Haldol eventually did its job. I had spent my entire life praying for a sign of God's existence, His investment in my soul, some reason for all this suffering, so even though sanity returned, I was still very confused about this whole Jesus trip. If Jesus or Moses or Abraham lived today, I wondered, would they not get locked up in a mental institution all the same? I had received a profound message of love, one that transcended all religious dogma: that God was real and His love was good and we didn't need to wait until we got to heaven to know it either. *Doesn't God's truth still need to be heard?* I asked myself. *What if this is His purpose for me?*

After a little more time and medication, I was able to fully drop the savior bit. Now I was ready to start figuring out what had happened to my mind. I began attending some of the psychoeducational classes offered to patients. One of the psychiatrists stood up at the whiteboard in front of us and listed symptoms of manic psychosis. Of particular relevance was his review of grandiose delusions. He explained that some people thought they were famous, some thought they were rock stars, and some people became so grandiose that they believed themselves to be God reincarnated.

"Oh shit." I quickly raised my hand. "That happened to me!"

Up until this point, the verdict was still out as to what was really going on. Clearly, I had been psychotic, but my history of drug and alcohol abuse blurred the diagnostic criteria for bipolar disorder and schizophrenia. I was given more information and found out that manic psychosis often included many if not all of my experiences. Delusions, euphoria, paranoia, grandiosity, sleeplessness, restlessness, agitation, hyperreligiosity, hypersexuality, increased substance abuse—these were all symptoms of my last few weeks in Athens, if not my entire adolescence. I was relieved to just have a chemical imbalance in my brain. For a second there, I'd thought I was an alcoholic.

Chapter 21

CHEMICAL DEPENDENCE

They let me go after a week or so, but I had to begin outpatient treatment. I learned more about bipolar disorder, that it is a chronic, permanent brain disease requiring a lifetime of medication. They told me having bipolar was like having diabetes, and just as diabetics had to take insulin, I had to take psychotropics. Hearing that my mind was permanently damaged was a difficult pill to swallow. Harder was accepting that faulty brain chemistry, and not God, had been responsible for my recent revelations. The worst part was when they told me I should entirely avoid mood-altering substances.

Outpatient treatment was way worse than inpatient hospitalization. I had to go to hours of group therapy, where I was encouraged to talk about my feelings. *No thanks.* I didn't have any practice processing emotions, so the whole idea of crying in front of a bunch of strangers threatened my manhood. I was eager to put all this behind me. *I'm an optimist,* I thought. *This shit is depressing.*

There were many more women than men, and I suspected the other guy in my group was gay. He was always talking about the latest poem he'd written in his journal. There was nothing gayer than poetry, in my stereotypical, sheltered worldview. Generally, my group consisted of a bunch of adults, much older than I was, having a really hard time with problems that were way bigger than mine.

I just went crazy for a minute, I tried to convince myself. *I wasn't abused. I don't cut. I've never considered suicide. Compared to these people, I'm fine.*

After a few days, the Risperdal made me so tired that I could barely keep my eyes open. Even with copious amounts of coffee and diet soda, I was still having trouble staying awake. I started complaining to Dr. Simpson, and prior to the weekend, he prescribed me Lexapro, an antidepressant, to take in addition to the antipsychotic medication. He said that hopefully it would give me a little more energy. It worked.

The Spirit came on strong. I felt incredible—so clear, so grateful to be back to myself. *Man, that antidepressant worked fast*, I thought, while cranking out an hour of cardio on my parents' elliptical machine. *This whole medication deal isn't so bad!*

My friend Hanna, a girl from the neighborhood who was also at UGA, was home for the weekend and came over to see how I was doing. I was eager to tell her. "You know, I feel great. They gave me some meds and now I'm totally back to normal!"

On Monday, when I woke up to go back to the hospital, I was feeling even better. God was still taking care of me. I decided to put on my purple polo shirt as a sign of my divine royalty, and then I popped my collar for some added flair. I clipped my orange camera case to my belt, and carried in it my Bible and a few magical items, like cherry ChapStick to keep my speech pure, and my oversized Costa Del Mar sunglasses to block out any negative energy. I was geared up to go preach the good word of God to Ridgeview's sick and weary, and nothing would keep me down. I stood out on the front lawn, reading scripture aloud as patients entered the building, while my mom went inside to talk to the doctors about my apparent relapse.

I was so euphoric that it barely fazed me when they told me I had to get hospitalized again. Upon reentry, I immediately missed my schizophrenic roommate, since he would cosign my madness. My new roommate was detoxing off heroin, and boy, was he in a bad mood. When I showed him a drawing I made of him with my crayons and began telling him all about how he was going to be my royal bodyguard, he threw me to the ground, stood over me, pointed his finger in my face, and yelled, "Stay the fuck away from me, or I'll kill you!" Now I was certain Satan lived in the hospital with me; he was my roommate.

I somehow managed to go another week without getting murdered by the devil or locked in any padded rooms. Now that I'd had a manic episode that wasn't triggered by alcohol or drugs, it was official: I met all the diagnostic criteria for bipolar disorder. Being diagnosed with a mental illness, a lifelong condition with no cure, is really hard, but my parents were medical people, so they probably got it quicker than most. For them, the diagnosis brought some relief; they finally knew what was wrong with their son. But for me, a mere psychiatric label wasn't nearly enough to bring about any healing. I knew these waters ran deep, even if all the medical experts were content just to call me bipolar.

My treatment became exclusively geared toward mood management. Any ideas about addiction or alcoholism took a backseat to this trump card of a diagnosis. They did tell me I had to stop drinking and taking drugs, but at least my substance use wasn't the cause of my insanity. Substance abuse was a symptom, an attempt to self-medicate.

After completing my outpatient stint, I began seeing a psychologist-and-psychiatrist team for my continued care. Dr. Buford talked to me about life, and Dr. Layne prescribed me medicine. Together, they tried to teach me how to recognize symptoms, change my behavior, and accept my diagnosis. I wasn't ready to make any lifestyle changes, so I treated them like the long arm of my parents, listening to what they had to say but ultimately making up my own mind. I decided very quickly that I still wanted to be normal. I still wanted to drink.

During the first couple of months, I just wanted to feel better. I had become severely depressed, something my doctors explained was a normal part of recuperation after a manic episode. I really paid close attention to what they had to say. I didn't want to go crazy again. I learned as much as I could about bipolar and what sort of events triggered manic episodes. I figured out the basic pharmaceutical interventions and treatments. I even read a couple of books about my new disorder. I saw somewhere that patients could drink moderately, like one or two glasses of wine, so that made me feel better. There was still hope for normalcy.

Even amid the rapid digestion of information regarding the cognitive, mood, and behavioral implications of my condition, I couldn't stop contemplating my spiritual experiences. Regardless of my psychosis, I still believed that God had given me insight into His workings, and I had finally realized that Jesus wasn't a magician. He was a man, a lover of humanity, the perfect lover of humanity, because He understood God fully; nothing more, nothing less. I had never felt more sure of anything in my life, regardless of bipolar disorder. This was still important stuff to teach, I thought, and if I didn't share my insights with the world, wouldn't I be letting God down? Maybe Jesus had bipolar disorder too. He did sound confused at times. Maybe we shared a similar experience.

At this stage of my life, when I had total dependence on alcohol for my every social need, there was hardly a chance of compliance, especially if that meant sobriety. I remember sitting in the basement with Allison, talking to her about my experience, and bursting into tears: "They said I can't drink anymore." I should have been grieving a life-altering diagnosis, not worrying about whether I could drink beer at the next band party, but that was all I cared about. They were trying to take my only solution away from me.

I started to theorize the many ways in which I could have gone insane without actually being bipolar. Lexapro, which I had been given after my first hospitalization, was still a drug, even if it was a prescribed medication, so didn't that qualify for drug-induced psychosis? Maybe I just had a sensitive nervous system. I found a few articles online that showed sleep deprivation could cause psychosis, and a few others that talked about drug use and alcohol withdrawal. Maybe all those Red Bull-and-vodka drinks had kept me from sleeping, which in turn had prevented necessary REM cycles, which had eventually led to a state of consciousness in which my waking and dream lives merged into one. I decided I just needed to make sure to get enough sleep, that if I hadn't been up all night partying for weeks on end, my psychosis wouldn't have happened.

If Jesus had been psychotic, then maybe psychosis wasn't such a bad thing. Maybe, I thought, delusions are God's way of altering the course of humanity. Maybe what is considered to be a delusion today was considered a revelation back in Jesus's time.

The lithium was supposed to give me clarity, but I had never been more confused. God had brought me up to heaven and then dropped me on my ass. I had just experienced an exchange with God more intimate than anything I'd ever thought possible and was now being told my revelations were merely the result of swirling brain chemicals.

I guessed God really did work in mysterious ways, because no matter how hard I tried, I couldn't figure out what the hell He was asking of me.

Chapter 22

BLAMING BIPOLAR

I was eager to get back up to Athens and put all this behind me. If I did everything the doctors told me, and I didn't have any setbacks in my treatment, I would be able to return to the University of Georgia for the spring semester. Not to return as soon as possible meant a kind of death, one in which I had no friends, would never attract a partner, and might be forever branded as a psychopath. My departure from school felt like a public-relations nightmare, and I desperately needed to protect my image, lest everyone think I was permanently insane. I needed to go back and prove that I was still the same person, that my altered reality had been just a bump in the road.

I met with Dr. Buford or Dr. Layne weekly leading up to my return. We spent most of our time talking about my plans for success upon reentering the college scene. The main ingredients were study, sleep, diet, and exercise. We didn't talk at all about the general themes of my psychosis. We didn't mention my body obsession, my sexual shame, my penile dysmorphia, my unrequited love for Chloe, or my existential angst around death and religion. We didn't talk about why I might have thought I was Jesus other than that grandiosity and delusions were part of bipolar disorder. We made calendars, set goals, and wrote out agreements with my folks on how they were willing to support me in my college aspirations. It was all very logical. We stared at the tip of the iceberg, either unaware of or unwilling to engage the deeper psychological discomfort lurking beneath the surface.

I had every intention of taking my sanity seriously. I promised my parents and my doctors that I would stay under control. To them, I agreed to stay sober, and in my mind, I would drink only socially, a beer or two here and there. I would no longer get drunk. I wouldn't smoke pot or do other drugs either. Our plan was for me to take nine credit hours in order to ease back into the academic workload. I would put off any thoughts about joining a fraternity until next fall. The need to regain normalcy motivated me to some extent. I planned my exercise and diet regimen with renewed hope and practiced positive thinking. *I can do this. I can do this. I can do this.*

I had gained a lot of weight, and so it was hard to differentiate depression from body shame. Perhaps body shame was a coping mechanism, some way for me to stay distracted. There was a long list of events I tried not to think about. In my first semester at college, I'd lost my virginity, told everyone I was Jesus, gotten arrested in my dormitory, made the school newspaper, and forfeited my scholarship. I was not in a fraternity, and Chloe surely thought I was a psycho. So much was out of my control, but I had power over my body. All I really needed to do was diet, exercise, and have a little faith.

Leading up to my return to Athens, my depression gained momentum with each passing week, and my body's demise followed suit. I had no energy, and so I couldn't work out, and because I couldn't work out, I had no energy. The more depressed I felt, the more ashamed I was of my body, and the more ashamed I was of my body, the more depressed I felt. This made me emotional, and so I would eat, and because I would eat, I was more emotional. After gaining about thirty pounds of self-hatred, I decided lithium wasn't going to work for me.

When Dr. Layne switched me to Depakote, he explained that antipsychotic and mood-stabilizing pharmaceuticals often had the side effect of weight gain. So I stopped taking them. I found out the lithium alternatives didn't require blood levels, and if I wasn't getting tested, there was no way for my doctors to prove whether or not I was complying with treatment. I barely cared about the risk involved; I just didn't want to be fat again.

I would go to great lengths to pretend I was taking my medicine. I described my mood and all the changes I imagined my doctors were looking to see. I would go to CVS and pick up my prescriptions, and then I would dump the previous bottle at the gas station, just to make sure my parents wouldn't discover a bottle full of pills rattling around in their trash can.

I thought the medication had made me depressed, since it certainly had made me very tired. When I stopped taking the medication, though, the depression remained, and the anxiety worsened. All the caffeine in the world couldn't cure me of my postmanic lethargy. After I complained about my depression a few times to Dr. Layne, he agreed to put me on an antidepressant, Wellbutrin, in addition to the Depakote I was pretending to take. To make matters worse, in the weeks remaining before my return to school, I started popping diet pills again, desperately hoping to enhance my mood and energy. I knew I was playing with fire, since stimulants were a big no-no and an antidepressant had previously landed me in the hospital, but if I took the mood stabilizer, I might gain more weight, and above all else, I couldn't have that.

When I got back up to Athens for the spring, I moved into an apartment with one of my high-school classmates, Brent, who was taking classes at a local community college in the hopes of eventually transferring to UGA. It felt incredibly painful and embarrassing to be around my peers again. In every interaction, I wondered how much people knew about what had happened to me, if they'd witnessed my break directly, and what they were thinking of me now. It was anxiety, bordering on paranoia. I needed to get drunk.

I truly did want to control my drinking, but I blacked out the first night away from my parents. Brent didn't even know me very well, since we'd run with different crowds in high school, so it was an awkward situation. When I woke up the next morning, the left side of my face ached. After some prodding on my part, Brent delicately filled me in on the evening. It turned out I'd gotten unruly with a handful of his friends. They were all on guard, having heard rumors of my recent insanity, and one of them decided to knock me out cold when I wouldn't "calm down."

In no time, I was back to my old self. The days were spent sporadically attending class, getting high, and playing hours of video games. Poker tournaments, barhopping, and frat parties occupied my nights. I began the semester sure that I would stick to my workout routine, but I sprained my ankle a couple of times walking drunk over curbs, so I couldn't exercise to my satisfaction. I spent the majority of the semester in an ankle brace, and even when I could work out again, I had gained so much weight that I was too anxious to go to the gym.

Prior to this point, I was familiar with blacking out, but totally losing all recollection of the previous night was now a near certainty. It's a wonder I stayed alive. Brent would come home and find me passed out in the living room to *Family Guy* DVDs, in front of half-smoked bowls of weed and boxes of delivered food. One time, Brent had to pay off a pizza delivery guy when he found me inebriated, shoving the delivery guy out the door, refusing to pay for my party-sized order of pepperoni rolls.

I started skipping classes more often, mostly due to my social anxiety from the continued weight gain. Alcohol withdrawal and marijuana-induced paranoia might have had something to do with it as well. When I did attend, I would profusely sweat on my way there and have near panic attacks once inside the classroom. Then, a few days prior to the deadline for dropping classes, I dropped all but one class, leaving me with only three credit hours of English, and I didn't tell a soul.

I smoked pot every day and got drunk every night. My anxiety got so bad that I stopped attending my one remaining class entirely. I didn't even leave my apartment unless it was absolutely mandatory. Brent would make calls to Jason, telling him that he hadn't seen my face in days. He'd have to knock on my bedroom door to make sure I was okay. Sometimes, I wouldn't even open the door; I'd just yell, "I'm sleeping!"

I kept gaining weight, living off delivery and fast food and sleeping until the afternoon. I was so socially anxious and fearful of what people thought about my rapid weight gain that even when I was drunk, I hoped that my friends would opt to stay in for the evening and just play poker. I especially wanted to avoid running into any girls I knew, most notably Chloe.

As the semester came to an end, I knew I was going to have to come clean to my parents. We talked almost every day, but all I ever told them was that I was depressed. No one knew I had dropped my courses or that I hadn't gone to class in a month. Brent was my only roommate, and he was gone all day for his own classes. I went home a few times for my doctors' appointments and lied to them too. My weight gain was seen as a symptom of depression and a side effect of my medication. We brainstormed ways for me to get more active and eat healthier. I would always leave a little hopeful, but I was too far gone, and health seemed completely out of reach.

I'd been a very bad boy, and it was only a matter of time before my parents would ask to see my report card. The thought that maybe my level of inactivity, reclusiveness, disordered eating, substance abuse, and existential turmoil might be contributing to my suffering was something I generally ignored and often repressed. Better to blame bipolar disorder, and so it became my excuse. When the semester ended, I confessed to my parents that I had been morbidly depressed, even more so than I had let on, hoping they would sympathize upon receiving the looming news of my elaborate deceptions.

Chapter 23

INTO THE WILD

I imagined everyone was judging me—for my weight gain, for my psychosis, and for my general lack of success. I didn't want to be judged. My religious views were mostly retired, and I considered whether or not I was even still a Christian. I became bitter. I no longer believed in miracles, and I grew skeptical, imagining that every prophet of the Bible was merely psychotic. If I wasn't allowed to have my revelations, then they shouldn't either. I was no longer a virgin, not in any sense of the definition. I was fully untethered, floating in space, desperately searching for a reference point, any sign that God or His universe still cared.

I was unable to concern myself with things that used to matter a great deal. My major was premed, but I didn't want to be a doctor anymore. I didn't even want to study science at all. Everything I did seemed so small and insignificant. Life took on a lame look. All I really wanted to do, all I really could do, was contemplate God. I felt so alone in my spirituality, as if the universe had told me a secret and I had to keep it to myself. Jesus wasn't really born of a virgin. I wanted to tell everyone, but if I talked about God, they would all just think I had gone insane again. Everything seemed so pointless.

It wasn't that I necessarily denied having bipolar disorder, but I definitely refused the treatment. The spiritual sensations that accompanied my mania were too real to ignore. I felt a kinship with the prophets, regardless of how insane my episodes appeared. Moses and Noah had fared just fine without psychotropics, and I could too.

While I was busy deifying my diagnosis, my parents were grieving. They learned about the horrible manifestations of bipolar disorder, and they researched various ways to help. When I got home, they suggested that I go on a wilderness course, and I agreed that a change of scenery might do me some good. If nothing else, it would help me lose a little weight.

The National Outdoor Leadership School provided an opportunity for students to earn college credit during wilderness excursions throughout the world. I selected their original program, a thirty-day course in the Wind River Range of Wyoming, a beautiful landscape with miles of forests and mountains carved out by rivers and streams. It seemed like the ideal setting, the perfect destination where I could figure out what I really wanted to do with my life.

I left for the great outdoors, destined to forge meaning in this rapidly changing existence. I took my journal, a month's supply of antidepressants, and an unmarked bottle of diet pills. If there was any hope for me, it would be in the middle of the wilderness, clean and sober, with an opportunity to reconnect with Spirit.

I was pleased to discover that my cohort wouldn't include any girls, since an all-male group gave me the best chance of going thirty days without an anxiety attack. Over a dozen of us and two instructors left the base with only the bare essentials for survival. The simplicity of the trip was refreshing, since my life had been consumed by extraneous details, and I wondered if part of the success of the prophets was that they lived in simpler times. We would wake up and go to bed with the sun. We would live by fire and hike all day. We brought fishing poles and sleeping bags and tents. No phone, no television, no video games, no Internet.

The first day of hiking scared me to death. It was raining. We took a straight line up the muddy slope toward our destination, and I wondered whether I would be able to last the full thirty days without needing a helicopter rescue. I noticed that I was the fattest guy on the trip, which didn't make me feel better about my prospective success. Lucky for me, there was a younger guy who had a really hard time. If it hadn't been for his constant complaining and demanding breaks, I don't know if I would've made it. Every time he stopped the group, I said a little prayer of thanks.

Over the course of a few days, and certainly within the ensuing weeks, I started to feel like myself again. My energy was restored, and I began to enjoy the hikes. The scenery was majestic, and it turned out that the wilderness provided healing all on its own. I became convinced that humans were made to exist in their natural habitat. Modern civilization was a prime culprit, breeding infirmity and psychological discomfort. Man needed to move, to enjoy space, to be free of the distractions and constant stimulation inherent in our modern times.

I began to feel successful again. Each mountain summited served as a reminder that I was capable of achieving greatness once more. I could tell that I was losing weight. We didn't have any mirrors, but my clothes fit looser, and I was certainly more vibrant. My body was getting back in shape, my mental efforts were easier, and I just knew that God was working with nature to heal me. My every thought turned to Him. He would confirm my secrets and encourage me to live a better life. I swore to Him that when I got back, I wouldn't do drugs anymore. I would exercise and eat right. I was going to live a good life in His honor.

Not only was I feeling restored, I was inspired by the great wisdom nature had to offer. In nature, everything was simple, and nothing was wasted. I could see God in the trees, in the riverbeds, in the interconnectedness of ecology. I would sit by the river and listen, considering how much time it had taken for the water to carve out the land. In the depths of my being, I knew my proper place in space and time, and through the small speck of my existence shone God's infinite light. The beauty of this world astonished me. For the first time in my life, I could feel my wealth. God was good.

It's amazing what thirty days in the wilderness will do to the senses. I couldn't wait for the simple pleasures of life. I eagerly awaited the sound of music, the taste of food, the joy of a movie. My fellow travelers and I planned our return. We would all go to a pizza place and peruse the tiny downtown of Lander, Wyoming. I didn't forget the promises I'd made to God and the rules for righteous living I'd recorded in my journal. I would be better this time. The rules were easy: eat well, exercise, and stay off drugs. God was automatic, so long as I kept my body right.

Despite my good intentions, when we got back, I was irresistibly enticed to drink beer and pack in some chewing tobacco. I still had my fake ID. *Beer is fine; Jesus drank wine*, I thought to myself. *Plus, tobacco is a plant; the Native Americans used it for rituals.* I didn't overdo it at least. I had two beers, and that was enough. I was still going to be fine. I would still lead the righteous life. I wouldn't let God down this time.

When I got home, my parents agreed to let me spend the night at a high-school friend's house. I was ecstatic to have lost over thirty pounds during my trip, and I was feeling good enough to be social again. Jason, Henry, and some of my other buddies who went to different colleges had grown concerned over the last year, having seen my drinking get so out of control and knowing what I'd been through, so I was excited to report to them my new plan of healthy living. Of course, this was all over a keg of beer. When I woke up the next morning, I was shocked to realize I had blacked out again. Henry asked me, "Didn't you say you weren't going to get drunk anymore?"

"I wasn't that drunk," I retorted. "I think my tolerance is just low from being away for so long."

The next day, my parents sat me down. They had gotten my grade report in the mail, and it showed that I had lied and taken only three credit hours the whole spring semester. I was relieved to hear that I had passed my course, but they were obviously discouraged.

They pleaded with me: "Chris, you have a brain disorder. No, it's not ideal, but it could be much worse." They pointed out that Dr. Layne said there was nothing I couldn't do, with proper treatment. They couldn't even imagine how hard this must be, they told me, but there was no excuse for such extreme deception. "We're on your team, Chris," they said. "You have to tell us the truth."

I was so ashamed. All I could do was all I had ever done: bawl my eyes out and promise to change. I told them how I'd seen the light, how my time in the wilderness had given me new perspective, how I was ready to be the son they wanted me to be. I believed I could change, that I could control my drinking and stop using drugs by just making a decision, by just caring more.

I was feeling better, so I think the good news of my improved mood offset their rage. Regardless, they were very disappointed, and after much deliberation, they decided that though I would be allowed to return to the University of Georgia, it would be on the strictest of terms. With the help of Dr. Buford and Dr. Layne, we worked out a behavioral contract, the stipulations for what we called my "parent scholarship." I was confident in my ability to return to form, and I assured them that their faith in me would be rewarded.

Chapter 24

CHASING NORMAL

The wilderness had healed me. I couldn't explain it, but I just knew it to be true. I was now free to pursue college as originally planned. I promised God, my parents, my doctors, and myself that I would do better this time. I had my plan of attack. I would eat right and exercise regularly. I would drink only on weekends. I would stay away from drugs. I would go to class and turn in all assignments. Mom and Dad had me on a tight leash, but I think they were happy to see me feeling better. As long as I made a 3.0 GPA and stayed out of trouble, I could have my life back.

My sophomore year was like the freshman year I didn't get to have. I moved into an apartment with Jason just outside of campus, and a few of our high-school friends and his fraternity brothers lived in the same complex. I was reunited with my bestie, and my sense of having a little community, combined with Jason's decision to live with me, affirmed that I didn't need to join a fraternity after all.

For the most part, I kept my life together, but it wasn't long before I returned to regular drug and alcohol use. I would wake up, go to class, exercise, and then get high or drunk as my reward for a job well done. My mood hinged on a carefully crafted cocktail of diet pills, antidepressants, marijuana, and whiskey. Chasing the next fix felt like a never-ending game of Whac-A-Mole, in which one addiction popped up the moment I took care of another.

Any spirituality that had started to form in the wilderness was replaced with a hedonistic philosophy, holding pleasure as its primary principle. It was all God's fault. If He hadn't made me like this, then I wouldn't act this way. If something felt good, how could it be wrong? *This is just my nature,* I told myself. I used my self-gratifying logic to justify further sexual promiscuity, substance abuse, and the general lack of concern for my health. *"Eat, drink, and be merry."* Not a lot had changed. I was still just adopting whichever philosophy best suited my behavior.

I decided to change my major to housing and economics. The only real reason I picked this particular major was because it seemed easy, and I didn't have to apply for acceptance. I figured I could flip houses for a living, even though I didn't know the first thing about it. The path of least resistance gave me the best opportunity to stay sane. I didn't want the stress of applying myself and possibly being disappointed. At this stage of the game, I merely needed to get by without losing my mind. If I could simply stay stress-free and get enough sleep, I might avoid going crazy and keep my parents off my back. I just wanted to be normal.

None of my friends seemed to be struggling the way I was, even though I rarely drank alone. I couldn't understand why I was so different. Their ability to stop drinking short of catastrophe caused great jealousy for me, and I would secretly revel in their embarrassment any time one of them acted out of line. I compared myself to others as a way of normalizing my behavior, and every arrest, every blackout, every sexual mishap on their part served to validate that I was not alone in my dysfunction. Each blunder was labeled "normal college behavior," and I grew numb to it all.

My relationship to substance abuse gained a great deal of complexity. Before my first drink, I would get my buddies to hide my debit card and car keys to give myself the best chance of staying out of jail. I would go downtown with just my fake ID and enough cash for a few drinks. I was always hammered before I even left my apartment, lest some social situation throw me into a panic. The next morning, when my friends would all get together, I was like a detective trying to figure out what kind of mess I had gotten myself into the night before. Most of the time, I pretended to remember. There's no telling how many nights I lost to blackouts, and my lack of recollection critically deepened my shame.

Even though I spent nearly every waking moment chasing the next high, I still couldn't avoid the voice in my head that was calling me to higher action. I had a strong guilt complex, and at night, in the event that I was still conscious, I would ask God for forgiveness. I couldn't see a way out. I was too weak to change, and God seemed overly ambivalent about my case. I believed that He was punishing me, possibly for sins in a previous life. By my estimation, He had been punishing me for as long as I could remember. At times, I felt like God owed me an apology, but then I would immediately apologize. You don't challenge God; everyone knows that.

Some aesthetic improvements to my body helped ease the angst. The weight loss from my wilderness excursion gave me a nice boost toward regaining my recently squandered physique. Body fixation was my go-to neurosis, and so I made it my mission to get back in shape. If I could just get back to my high-school weight, then life would return to normal. I begged my parents to buy me some free weights and an exercise bike for my apartment, a wish they were more than happy to grant. Any move toward health was always met with great support and enthusiasm.

One night, a few of my friends went downtown as usual, and we got stopped by a couple of police officers for jaywalking. I was twenty years old and so used to underage drinking that it never even occurred to me that I was doing anything illegal. The fact that I was still coherent at all gave me an added boost of confidence. I was shocked to hear an officer abruptly ask us, "Have you boys been drinking?"

"Yessir," I kindly replied, expecting to continue on my way.

"Let me see some identification," he barked.

And just like that, I was arrested for being a minor in possession of alcohol.

Here I was again. More probation. More attorney fees. More disgust from my parents. More behavioral contracts. The only reason they let me go back to school was the hope that I might be able to graduate and turn my life around with a college degree. I blamed it all on bipolar disorder. I was self-medicating with drugs and alcohol. None of it was my fault. I even convinced myself that my blackouts were the result of mixing my antidepressant with alcohol, rather than the result of my overconsumption.

I openly discussed drinking with my doctors for the first time. I didn't really have a choice. I told them that I had a difficult time stopping once I started. I didn't admit to any drug use, and I kept my diet pills a secret. I also didn't confess that I was off my mood stabilizer and taking only my antidepressant. Upon the news of my arrest, Dr. Buford and I agreed that I would commit to a year of sobriety. As insurance, Dr. Layne prescribed me Antabuse, a daily medication that when combined with alcohol produced severe illness, nausea, and vomiting.

Life improved once I got sober. My grades went up. I went to class more often. I was less moody. My social anxiety didn't get any better though, and I nearly stopped going out altogether. I used the opportunity to get even more obsessive with my diet and exercise regimen. By my estimation, I still had about twenty pounds to lose. I adopted a strict diet of protein powder and peanut butter, except for a foot-long Subway sandwich I allowed myself after weight-lifting sessions. I stymied any hunger pangs with copious amounts of Fresca. Once again, I was a machine.

Junior year rolled around, and attaining my ideal weight brought about a difficult realization: I was still miserable. My anxiety shifted from my body to my career. *What do I really want to do in life? What is my calling?* I started talking to my parents about how I didn't think UGA was for me, and they were very supportive. I had always excelled at science and math, and we'd all thought that I would be a doctor or a dentist. Housing and economics and flipping properties never really sounded like my thing.

Ever since I'd started dieting and working out in high school, I had been obsessed with health and fitness. At the suggestion of my parents, and after some research, I set my sights on Life University, a school fewer than ten miles from home, best known for its doctor of chiropractic program. Even though it was known for its graduate training, it had an undergraduate school as well. Specifically, Life University offered a joint-degree program, where students could earn both their undergraduate degree and their Doctor of Chiropractic degree simultaneously. It seemed to be the perfect move.

My parents were happy to see me out of Athens, and my friends didn't really argue, having seen how out of control I had been for a couple years now. I moved back in with my parents and started taking accelerated undergraduate courses, science prerequisites for the chiropractic school.

It was way easier than Georgia, and living at home with my parents ensured that I could keep my priorities in check. It was like being back in high school. I would get all of my work done before class each day, and my evenings consisted of naps, working out, and dinner with the family.

I stopped taking Antabuse, deciding that I didn't really have a drinking problem anymore, which was convenient, since I was ready to drink again. On the weekends, I would often head up to Athens to party for a couple of days and stay with friends. I was still managing to embarrass myself. On my twenty-first birthday, Chloe's boyfriend punched me in the face because I wouldn't stop hitting on her at the bar. It had been years since we were close, but I was still obsessed.

Once I was twenty-one and could legally drink, my parents viewed my drinking as slightly less of an issue. For years, I had contended that my chief problem was that I was acting *illegally* by drinking, not that I was necessarily acting *alcoholically*, a vital distinction that only occasionally made rational sense. Despite my frequent road trips, I managed to stay out of trouble and began slowly earning back the trust of my parents. They could see a real change in me. I was living under their roof, making good grades, and exercising regularly. I could feel a real change in myself.

I started reading a lot of self-improvement books. Much of my reading was helping me settle into a newfound spirituality. My whole Jesus psychosis had left a bad taste in my mouth around religion. Not only did I start to think that there was something psychologically tragic about religion, but I also felt like an outsider. I blamed some of my Christian beliefs for my manic episode, convinced that if it hadn't been for my fantastical views on God, I might have avoided psychosis entirely.

I did my best to untangle religion and spirituality, hoping to stay close to God despite my inability to trust biblical mythology. I relied solely on my personal revelations, trusting that a personal relationship with God would be enough to heal me of my sins and set me on a more righteous path. Maybe these past couple of years were what my consciousness needed to evolve. Maybe psychosis was my soul's way of breaking through, of setting me on a different course.

I became kind of a self-help nut, reading whatever I could find about spirituality, psychology, exercise, and dieting. I even read a book about being an enlightened entrepreneur. I was all over the place, but I felt like I was headed in the right direction. I was in good shape. I got good grades. I was redefining my relationship with God. I even started trying to meditate. I was a good boy again.

Chapter 25

CALLING COSMIC CHRIS

A flier came in the mail advertising a new Dahn Yoga studio near our house. Dahn Yoga claimed to combine yoga, tai chi, and energy healing. The flier promised increased energy, mood, flexibility, weight loss, happiness, and peace of mind. My dad gave it to me, suggesting I should check it out since I was showing such a passion for alternative spiritual pursuits. The studio was right around the corner. It was destiny.

I called for the free mandatory initial consultation and energy-healing session. A fit, vibrant, middle-aged Asian lady greeted me at the door. She was the studio's "Dahn master." Her name was Miwa, which she told me meant "beautiful flower." She had me lie down and started moving her hands slowly above my body. She barely spoke English. When she ran her hands above my abdomen, she stopped and asked, "Surgery?"

I was stunned. Was she asking about my liposuction? Maybe she was asking about my appendectomy when I was a little boy. Either way, the fact that she could tell I had surgery, through my clothes, without even touching me, was startling to say the least. She had supernatural powers. It reminded me of Jesus.

When I looked confused, she didn't push the issue. Was she reading my mind? Did she know I didn't want to talk about it? Could she tell I was ashamed? There was something incredibly powerful about her. She hardly spoke at all, but the way she looked into my eyes was nothing short of mystical. *She must be psychic*, I thought. Then she touched my abdomen for a few seconds and said, "You drink alcohol." Miwa's hands were so hot that I wondered if she was wearing an electric device. When she removed her hands, the warmth of her touch lingered on my belly.

As we finished the body scan, Miwa started telling me about how she'd become a Dahn master. She was from Korea. Her husband had died and left her a widow. She told me how she'd become lonely and severely depressed, how she then began drinking and smoking a lot of cigarettes. One day she saw an advertisement for Dahn Yoga in the newspaper, an event she considered to be a sign from the universe. Once she attended, her life was miraculously transformed. She committed to becoming a master, spent the next six years training, and now she was living her purpose as the head of a Dahn Yoga center, spreading health and happiness to America. Her enthusiasm piqued my interest. I wanted some of that.

I was going through a rough time, but I wasn't suicidal, and I hadn't lost a spouse. If Dahn Yoga could turn her life around, it could certainly help me. I didn't tell her that I had bipolar. I didn't tell her anything about myself, other than that I was a chiropractic student. I felt like she knew me, like she could see through me into my soul. She didn't need the details; I was sure of that. In our short conversation and her brief introduction to energy healing, I began to speculate that bipolar disorder was just an energy imbalance. Perhaps this yoga stuff could cure me.

My parents were happy to see me pursuing any healthy activity, so they helped me sign up for a membership. It just seemed like an expensive gym contract. I was given an all-white uniform that looked like my childhood karate outfit. Students were encouraged to always wear the uniform to class in order to show solidarity and to help develop "good energy." *Energy* was a buzzword thrown around a lot, and later I would learn about the idea of *chi*. Basically, everything emitted chi—universal life force, or energy. The whole point of our practice at Dahn Yoga was to cultivate more chi and increase energy flow in our bodies. We longed to be a positive force in the world, to give off good healing energy to all people around us. This energy had the power to restore health and induce enlightenment.

I was totally weirded out by the first class. I had never been to a yoga class before; I'd never even heard of tai chi, so it was all new to me. I didn't even know anything about Eastern spirituality except for what I'd read from Eckhart Tolle. Each class was exactly the same. Our classes were never very big. The most we would have would be about ten students at a time, and that was rare. I was one of two men; the other guy was older, probably in his fifties. Miwa told me privately that he had a difficult time progressing because he had too many ideas about spirituality already. She taught me about having a "beginner's mind," coming to class with a blank slate, a willingness to let go and learn.

We began by stimulating our *dan tien*, the main energy center of the body, located beneath the naval. We would hit our fists against this area while bouncing up and down. We would tap our entire body in order to stimulate the *meridians*, the anatomical paths that chi traveled throughout the body. Sickness was attributed to blockages in chi flow. We would tell our body parts how much we loved and appreciated them; we'd rub our knees and verbally express our gratitude. We'd chant about being healthy and happy, encouraging our bodies to cooperate.

After warm-ups, we would stretch and perform exercises, often holding various stances to maximize energy flow. Master Miwa stood at the front of the class, before a large mural of a field of flowers, and intuited which exercises we would perform. There would always be meditation, where we would hold our hands in front of our chest, visualizing and feeling an "energy ball" as we concentrated on our breath. We were instructed to feel the energy expand and contract as we breathed in and out. I could feel it. The chi was real. To finish the exercises, we would all lie down as Master Miwa provided energy healing. How'd she make her hands so warm? She was absolutely a master.

Finally, we would have a ritual tea ceremony at the end of each class. Everyone gathered in a circle over some "special" tea to share our experience from our time together. Some women would be incredibly moved about something that had happened, a thought they'd had, or a memory that had been triggered by the energy flow. In the beginning, I just talked about how easy or hard particular exercises were. It wouldn't be long before I was really "sharing" as well. The tea was supposed to increase the chi flow after class. I had never had hot tea before. It was all so foreign to me.

I particularly liked how good I felt after my individual energy-healing sessions with Master. After a weekend of partying, I'd go see her, and she would balance me out. She would talk to me about my drinking. She said that the more I came to class, the less I would need to use alcohol. There was really something to this energy-healing stuff; I could feel a major difference after each session. I wondered how long it would take for me to quit drinking.

After a few weeks, chi was always on my mind. Miwa encouraged me to do the warm-up exercises all throughout the day. The more I did them, the more positive chi I would experience. I woke up and did push-ups, sit-ups, and chi exercises. While I was sitting in school, I performed breath-work to stimulate my dan tien. Everything I ate, every thought that went through my mind, every movement, every encounter with another person occasioned an evaluation of how much chi I was absorbing, emanating, and enjoying. Energy was all around. The universe spoke in the language of chi, and I was becoming fluent.

My parents were encouraged by my newfound interest in yoga. I seemed to be more positive, more loving, and generally in a better mood. They had every reason to believe I was on the right track. I still was going to see my psychologist and psychiatrist regularly. My grades were good. I was passing all the standard tests with flying colors.

I started losing interest in going to Athens on the weekends, and if I did go, I felt like I was going just to spread positive chi to all my friends. I was getting very powerful. I began hanging out with some young people who attended the Dahn Yoga center downtown. I attended classes at multiple locations. I was becoming a devout Dahn yogi. I could feel chi coursing through my meridians. I learned about chakras, and I knew mine were burning bright. I would even see flashes of colors during class; it was magic.

The more I went to class, and the more I traveled to other Dahn Yoga centers around Atlanta, the more connected I felt to the Dahn community. I went to a workshop led by the head of the entire eastern region of Dahn centers in the United States. She came over to me and touched my hands, and I felt a wave of electricity run through my body. After class, she asked to speak to me privately. She grabbed my hands, looked me in the eye, and exclaimed, "You have big, big energy! You become Dahn master one day?" I laughed. I was flattered. I always knew I was special.

I started coming early to help Miwa set up for class, and then I stayed afterward to help clean. She began asking me to lead warm-ups. Shortly after that, I started teaching parts of the class that I had memorized. I could feel my energy increasing the more and more I practiced. What began as tapping my abdomen turned into full-on punching. My chi was huge. I started being able to consistently see colors around the masters, specifically purple glowing off the top of their heads. When I asked Master Miwa about it, she encouraged me not to be concerned with auras. She said not to worry and explained that the reason I saw purple over her head during class was that she was harnessing universal chi to help her teach.

At the peak of my transformation, I went with my buddies on spring break to Destin, Florida. I was on a spiritual plane, and it made partying a whole lot more fun. I spent about five days drunk, stoned, and high on cocaine. There was a pool at the house we were renting, constantly full of drunk college kids. I imagined that I was healing all of them with positive energy, that I was blessing the water just by being in the pool. I was making them laugh, causing them to have such a good time. The next morning, when the pool was stained burnt orange with alcohol and urine, I imagined that it was just colored with the negative energy I'd withdrawn from their bodies. My powers were a secret between God and me, so I didn't tell anyone.

After my spring break extravaganza, it became difficult for me to sit still in school. I would practice my deep breathing, but I grew restless and bored. I took breaks to grab green tea from the cafeteria. I started skipping so I could aimlessly walk around campus. I would feel the chi in my feet as I walked around, each step against the earth grounding me and charging my body. I practiced proper posture for maximum chi flow. Everything was changing. The world was brighter. I believed with growing certainty that I was becoming enlightened.

Master Miwa began telling me about a special young people's retreat in Sedona, Arizona. I might have the chance to meet Dr. Ilchi Lee, the Dahn grand master, founder of Dahn Yoga. She had never mentioned Lee before. She said he was enlightened, that his chi was the most powerful in the world. She gave me a book he wrote, and asked me to feel its energy. She had me hold the book over my heart and put out my other arm for a muscle test. She then started pulling on my strong arm and said, "You see, very good chi!" Then she had me repeat the same exercise with a different book, and my arm went limp. "See?" she cheerfully insisted, proving that my chi was attracted to the grand master's writings.

When I read Dr. Lee's book, I found out that the universe had transmitted the revolutionary techniques of Dahn Yoga to him in the mountains of Korea. He had gone into the wilderness without food or water, determined to meet his death, and instead had become enlightened and was given the tools to heal the world with Dahn Yoga. The story sounded like how Jesus fasted for forty days and forty nights.

The masters acknowledged that some people thought Dahn Yoga was a cult, but they maintained that people fear what they don't understand. At this point, a normal person might have questioned what was going on, but I was already hooked. *What cult?* I could see auras. I could feel chi. I was in the best mood of my life. I was becoming enlightened. There was nothing to worry about at all.

It just so happened that the young people's retreat was on the same weekend as Easter, when my family planned to go on a beach trip. I was a little nervous asking my parents whether I could go to Sedona, but I decided their answer would speak for the universe. Although they took some time to consider my proposition, in the end they were happy to gift me a trip that encouraged my newfound healthy yoga lifestyle. If I wasn't already all in before my trip to Sedona, I certainly was after.

The Sedona retreat blew my mind. It was exhilarating to see so many young people into the same thing, trying to live a spiritual existence, and hoping to spread health and happiness to the world. I had finally found my people. We met Grand Master Ilchi Lee, an old man with a cane, who drove a big yellow Hummer around the property. He didn't seem too special to me, but I figured maybe he had lost some chi with age.

We did Dahn Yoga all day for three days. We ate food with lots of chi. When we took breaks, we were encouraged to go absorb the chi from these stone circles they called "vortexes" on the property. I was introduced to the youngest American Dahn master, and I heard his story about how he'd been transformed from an angry, insecure kid into a confident and joyful man. I started really considering that I would like to be a Dahn master. If I worked hard, I could be an even younger master than he was.

When I got back to Atlanta, I was more committed than ever to my practices. It was all I did. Even when I lifted weights, I imagined the heavy resistance was opening up my chakras. A bench press was now a heart chakra exercise. Squats were a way to develop my root chakra. Running was a way to stimulate all of my meridians. I began drinking green tea around the clock, in addition to my diet pills. I determined that I no longer needed antidepressants. I was healed.

Chapter 26

MASTER MIND

Master Miwa could see a change in me. She suggested I start coming to the studio twice a day. I went early, before school, at 5:00 a.m. Then I would go after school for my evening class. I was definitely on the fast track to enlightenment. It was a secret; my family and friends wouldn't understand. Enlightenment scared people who didn't understand. The only people who understood were the masters. I was encouraged to stay humble; humility cultivated more chi, and pride dissipated chi. Any disclosure of my spiritual progress would have surely been out of pride, a function of ego.

One morning, Miwa showed me a piece of paper with a bunch of symbols on it in a grid formation. She said it was an ancient secret chant, rediscovered by Grand Master Lee, to help cultivate chi and achieve enlightenment. Together, we started combining the chants with some yoga movements. Miwa and I would bow down to a stack of brochures, sending positive energy into the marketing material, before we went around to neighborhoods and placed fliers in random people's mailboxes. We were praying for the universe to guide the brochures, so that Dahn could save the world.

Master Miwa told me that the chant was very powerful, but I didn't fully believe it until, one morning, I got a sign from God. We were in the middle of one of our chants, and when I got to the symbol that looked like a cross, it lit up bright blue and knocked me backward onto the floor. The explosion of light was a sign, no doubt. I really was the Christ; I'd just never understood before.

When I told Miwa, she again assured me that it was normal to experience chi in colors. She told me that Jesus was enlightened, but that He was not the only one. I needed to remember that even though I was becoming enlightened, I was not alone. I felt comforted by her explanation. It's a lonely feeling, thinking you are the Second Coming. She assured me that there were many of us, that Christ was a vibration, not one person.

A weekend workshop was coming up, and Miwa said I was ready for it. For weeks, she had told me I wasn't ready, but apparently she could see how well I was progressing. I wasn't allowed to talk about the event. She told me to keep it secret so as not to ruin any other students' experience once it was their turn. She said the workshop would change my life forever.

The workshop was held over two days at another Dahn Yoga location in Atlanta. The first day, we introduced ourselves, practiced special Dahn Yoga moves, and did various healing exercises to each other. The practices were unusually intimate. The masters had us gaze into each other's eyes and silently communicate. We partnered up and telepathically exchanged chi. We gathered around one person at a time and sent chi into them with our hands. There were lecture-style classes as well, where masters taught us about creating an enlightened society.

When the first day ended, we were encouraged to remain silent before coming back to the workshop the next day. I lived with my parents, so I just did the best I could. I didn't tell my folks that I wasn't supposed to talk; I just kept conversation brief. I never disclosed any Dahn practices to my parents. They wouldn't understand. They were "asleep," unaware of issues of enlightenment. My job was just to be kind to them and hope that they would awaken through my vibration. I was so excited to go back the next day that I barely slept. It was like Christmas morning.

After testifying about each of our life transformations upon finding Dahn Yoga, everyone was feeling very open and vulnerable. There was just one more thing, a final ceremony. The masters turned off the lights, played music, and sent positive energy into us while we sat in chairs with our eyes closed. After quite some time, one of the masters grabbed a microphone and began guiding us in a long meditation. He had us shout out our shortcomings, labels, and prejudices; anything getting in the way of enlightenment. Eventually, he began chanting repeatedly, louder and louder, "You are enlightened! You are Jesus! You are Buddha!" He said it over and over again, getting louder and more emphatic each time he declared we were reincarnated deities. Joy swept over my being. I had attained Christ consciousness; I was enlightened.

When the ceremony was over, we all circled up to talk about our purposes in life. One of the masters disclosed that he'd decided he would become a master when he first attended this workshop many years ago. People shared how they would live their lives differently moving forward. One of the students was a cop, and she shared that she would try to send positive chi to all people she came in contact with; even when she wrote a ticket or arrested someone, she would do it with love. When it got to be my turn, I announced that I would become a Dahn master, that I would commit my entire life to the mission of Dahn Yoga. Everyone cheered.

Now that I knew my purpose in life, I just had to work out the details. The masters encouraged me to wait to tell my parents and not to leave school. They assured me that the path of becoming a Dahn master took a very long time, many years, and lots of practice. I was already enlightened, I figured, so I didn't really need to listen to their advice. I just needed to listen to the universe and follow my heart. I knew God was allowing me to progress faster than normal. The other masters might have made a choice, but I was chosen.

I went back to school the Monday after the workshop, but I lasted only about an hour before deciding to leave class. I'd made up my mind. I was going to become a Dahn master, and nothing was going to stop me.

One of my school friends asked me what was going on. "Chris, you seem so happy. What have you been up to?"

"I've been practicing yoga a lot," I gleefully reported.

I ran into another friend on my way to the parking lot. Perplexed, he asked, "Where are you going, man?"

I gave him a big hug. "I'm going to become a yoga master."

I wouldn't be coming back to Life University. The universe—God— had bigger plans for me.

I went to Dahn Yoga to share the good news. Miwa was happy for me, but she was fearful that my body wasn't ready for enlightenment. She asked me a bunch of questions about life and the universe and how determined I was that I was ready to become a Dahn master. After my lengthy soliloquy on universal love and the oneness of all religions, she affirmed, "You are becoming enlightened."

She called a master from another location, and we all three sat together to discuss my desire to join their way of life. The other master was very encouraging but warned me that my parents might not understand; he himself had been disowned by his own father. He said that Dahn masters had to devote their whole lives to the cause: "We are like monks, but the difference is that we live in the world instead of in retreat. Becoming a Dahn master is the highest and most difficult calling." I was ready. It was like all those ideas of becoming a priest were finally making sense to me. I knew I was called; I just didn't know what for, until now.

Ecstatic to be on the path of Dahn mastery, I finally understood what God wanted of me. My psychosis, my alcohol and drug history, my body: it was all just the universe's way of guiding me to exactly where I was right now. My thinking was on a new plane, a dimension I'd never known existed. I was enjoying a cosmic consciousness, a vast departure from my old self. I could understand what the universe desired for humanity—that we fulfill our destiny and live as a united society. Global enlightenment was inevitable, and as a Dahn master I was going to be at the epicenter of our cosmic evolution. I would heal the world and fulfill the prophecies foretold by all the great wisdom traditions from antiquity.

Sleep became difficult. I would stay up all night writing in my journal and drawing pictures, powerful descriptions and diagrams of enlightenment. I couldn't wait until 5:00 a.m., when I could go to see Miwa for our morning exercises. She started having me do chores around the studio. I was learning to be a humble student to my master. I pretended to be going to school; I wasn't ready to tell my parents I had quit. I would go hang out at the park and visit various Dahn Yoga locations. This went on for only a few days before I felt ready to talk to my parents about my vocational pursuits.

"Mom and Dad, we need to talk."

When we sat down, I told them that I wanted to become a Dahn master, that I had been really enjoying my practice, that it had changed my life, and I wanted to do it for a living. They took a more practical approach, encouraging me to finish school first. I refused. I told them I would not be going back to college. I was going to start working at Dahn Yoga, and I would eventually run my own studio as a master.

They calmly encouraged me to stay in school, unaware that I had already dropped out. I couldn't take the lying anymore, so I told them, "I know what I want to do; I've already dropped my courses. I'm not going back."

They were floored. In a matter of a few weeks, I had gone from pretty normal functioning, even promising improvement, to "enlightened." They asked me about my medications, and I told them that I didn't need my medicine: "I stopped taking it. I realized I'm not bipolar; I'm an indigo child. Psychiatry doesn't know anything about enlightenment."

I explained that people who are "asleep" are afraid of enlightened beings. I reminded them about what happened to Jesus upon His enlightenment, that He was the Son of God, and they killed Him for it. The doctors were trying to do the same to me. Western medicine was the new Pharisees, refusing to acknowledge subtle energy and vibration. There was never going to be heaven on earth or an enlightened society, so long as avatars were branded delusional and pumped full of psychotropics. "If Jesus Himself came back to earth," I said, "they'd lock Him up for life!"

My behavior had officially sounded the alarm. My parents scheduled emergency appointments with Dr. Buford and Dr. Layne. I didn't care; I was going to educate them. But when I told Dr. Buford about how I was enlightened, he seemed to find it amusing and let me know that I was definitely having a manic episode. What did he know? He was asleep, just like my parents. Dr. Layne wrote me a prescription for some antipsychotics and encouraged me to take them under my parents' supervision, to avoid having to be hospitalized.

Even though I was spouting off a ton of spiritual jargon about being enlightened, it was assumed that this was just due to my being manic and had little to do with my yoga practices. My parents let me go to Dahn Yoga to see Miwa for an energy-healing session. They didn't realize all these spiritual concepts and practices were contributing to my episode.

When I saw Miwa, she was very concerned. She asked if I had been sleeping and said that my energy was off. She had me lie down for the energy work. Afterward, she turned on some music and had me hold these two little vibrating squishy toys in each hand, created by Grand Master Lee, designed to balance the left and right hemispheres of the brain. I could feel the chi working its way from my hands to my head, culminating in a sort of cool fire emanating from my brain. I lay there, giggling to myself, until I needed to pee.

In the bathroom I saw a poster for Dr. Ilchi Lee's latest book. There was a picture of a little kid's hand inside a larger adult hand. I placed my hand up to the poster, surprised to discover that it fit perfectly inside the outline of the kid's hand. I knew immediately that the little kid's hand was mine, and that the larger hand was Grand Master Lee's. I was destined to become his successor, the head of Dahn Yoga. I would be the spiritual leader of the world.

When I went into the room with Miwa to do some exercises to help bring my energy down, I started becoming psychotic, or at least *more* psychotic. My body felt on fire, as if I could burst into light at any moment. I was carrying a rosary in my pocket, and I threw it down on the ground and then stomped on it, breaking the cross off the beads. The cross's removal from the beads was God's sign that I was no longer bound by the Church. Christianity had muffed my teachings enough, and it was time for me to stand alone.

As my nervous system continued to go haywire, I spontaneously became erect and started having delusions that Miwa was going to force me to have sex with her. I quickly considered whether God was trying to make me conceive a child with Miwa in order to fulfill some divine incarnation. I threw myself on the ground, both trying to rid myself of the boner and exhausted by confusion. She started laughing nervously and telling me to calm down. I yelled at her, "You're the devil!" Right then, my mom entered the studio. Disappointed, Miwa held her hands behind her back, looked down, and ordered, "Go with your mother, Chris." I had failed her.

Mom took me home, where she attempted to get me to rest and take my medication. I did try to relax, but there was no way I was going to take those evil pills.

Later that evening, Dad brought me a stack of about a hundred pages of material printed off the Internet claiming that Dahn Yoga was a cult. He was so upset, feeling partially responsible for not seeing the signs earlier.

"I'm sorry this happened, but you need to read this stuff, Chris," he insisted. "That grand master guy isn't even a real doctor. He's being sued for tax evasion, sexual abuse against female disciples, and even wrongful death during one of their master trainings."

I wouldn't hear any of it. I told him what the masters had explained to me early on, that anything could be called a cult.

"Anything involving time and money is a cult. Sports are a cult, Dad. Jesus was a cult leader. Every religion that's ever existed started as a cult!"

Chapter 27

HERO'S RETURN

My manic episode coincided with Mother's Day weekend. Since the whole family had already planned to take a celebratory trip a couple of hours north of Atlanta to Lake Burton, where my folks had recently built a second home, the holiday weekend served as a convenient excuse to keep me away from Dahn Yoga, and hopefully get me some sleep. My parents called Dr. Layne to see if there was anything they could do, short of spiking my smoothie with antipsychotics, but since I wasn't threatening violence, all they could do was pray that I'd come to my senses and consent to medication.

On the road trip up to the lake, we stopped at a restaurant for dinner. I hadn't been eating very much and had lost a good bit more weight throughout my Dahn training. The more enlightened I became, the less I needed to eat; I was surviving on the chi of the universe. Food was merely a formality at this point. My soul didn't need food; only my body did. I had become identified with my subtle energy, somehow untethered from my physical body and its incessant demands.

My parents encouraged me to eat, saying I would feel better on a full stomach. Perhaps they thought eating would calm me down. I played along, feeling fairly ambivalent about whether or not I would like to take care of this body of mine. I remember eating so much that even Mimi and Poppy were commenting on it. I must have had two entire meals to myself, plus dessert. I felt much more grounded afterward. I guess even in my manic psychosis, I still knew how to use binge eating to take the edge off. Maybe my nervous system needed more glucose. It was like a spiritual eating contest.

I thought I was feeling better, but paranoia set in, getting especially bad at night. I imagined that Dahn Yoga was going to try to have me killed, since I knew too much. Every painting and statue, all the artwork around the house, was endowed with energy that could have a potential healing or harming effect on my fragile system. I could feel the spirit of the paintings and sculptures; the figures' eyes came alive. I even believed some of the Dahn masters might be in the house.

My family didn't trust me to be alone. My mom slept at my side, to help me feel safe and ensure that I would rest. In the light of day, I felt so much better. The dark was where the devil lived. During the day, I was back to being joyous, free, and peaceful. We went on a hike to a nearby waterfall. *Lots of beautiful chi going on here*, I thought to myself. I started taking some of the chi from the running water into my body. It was rejuvenating. I began to trust that I would weather the storm.

Mimi offered to help me paint something for my mom for Mother's Day. I took out my pencil and a canvas, and I started drawing the outline of my masterpiece. I felt incredibly creative. The perfect idea immediately came to mind. I drew a picture of my mom smiling, pregnant, with my happy face in her belly. It was a depiction of her pregnancy, when I'd felt so grateful to be coming into the world. I could remember my body's formation and the deep love of my expecting mother.

When it was time for the family to hand out Mother's Day gifts, I could barely hold in my excitement. Mom burst into laughter at the sight of the cartoonish depiction of her pregnant, naked body with a smiley face inside her belly and peace signs and hearts painted all around her. I told her that I remembered how happy I was that she would be my mom. Despite my family's assurance that I couldn't possibly remember my embryonic life or my birth or conception, I let them know that my soul remembered it all. I was fully identified with Spirit, some subtle quality beyond my physical form, no doubt an aspect of my enlightenment. I accepted that they were skeptical. I could still comprehend how difficult it must be for them to grasp. They weren't on my level. "You'll see one day," I assured them.

The lake trip went smoother than one might have expected, but I was still obviously altered. When we got home, I insisted that I be able to return to Dahn Yoga. The masters were just scared of Dad, I concluded. They knew I was enlightened; they'd even said so themselves. They would know what to do. I just needed to see them; they could help me calm down my energy. But my parents would hear nothing of it.

The night we got back, I started accusing my parents of holding me hostage against my will. When I told them I was leaving, they refused.

"I'm not sick. I'm not bipolar. I'm enlightened. You don't understand!"

They hid my car keys, informing me that it wasn't safe for me to drive.

"I'll walk then," I bluffed. "You can't stop me."

I began devising my plan of escape. A phone was mounted on the wall of my parents' bathroom. I pretended to need to use their restroom and then dialed 911 and left the phone disconnected. It would be just a matter of time until the police arrived, and I could then tell them about how my parents had kidnapped me and were holding me hostage. The cops could set me free. My heart was racing. It felt like an enormous gamble, since the police might be evil, but it was a risk I was willing to take for my freedom.

When the officer got to the house, my parents were shocked.

"What did you do, Chris?" my mom asked, wondering if I was getting arrested for something she didn't know about yet.

I informed her of my predicament: "You two are holding me against my will. You left me no choice. I'm reporting you to the cops."

I went running outside to tell my story, but my dad was already talking to the officer.

The cop yelled for me to stand back: "Son, do not come any closer!"

I complied.

I watched as he and my dad conversed at the end of our driveway, and before I could have a word with the officer, he got in his car and left. In my mind, either Dad had manipulated the cop or the police were in cahoots with Dahn Yoga or whatever governmental agency was trying to conceal my enlightenment.

"What did you tell him? You can't keep me here! Just take me to the hospital. I'll show you. I'm not crazy."

It wasn't nearly as bad to be in the hospital now that I knew I was just enlightened. This time, I was armed with tools. I could move my energy. I could meditate. I could do yoga. I could practice tai chi. This time, I was on a mission: convince the doctors to release me on the grounds of my enlightenment. I was going to save the world, but first I had to get the doctors' blessings. This proved more difficult than I imagined, especially since I was refusing medication. I bombarded them with questions instead: "Do you believe God is a delusion? Do you think Jesus was psychotic? Was Moses just hallucinating when he saw a burning bush?"

I started practicing my tai chi routine in the public area. It tickled me greatly to watch the staff prepare for my eventual attack, unaware of my peaceful disposition. It obviously looked like I was performing some sort of fighting demonstration, so they were smart to consider it a threat of violence, but it made me feel giddy, like I was engaging in some childish rebellion. It stoked familiar feelings of laughing in church or joking around in school. I felt like a little boy, free and playful, amused at the adults and all their rigidity and silly rules.

One of their large staff members told me sternly, "Please stop your karate moves; you're scaring other patients."

"It's nonviolent," I insisted, giving a salute. "Stand down, sergeant."

I continued my tai chi exercises in the privacy of my room, imagining myself to be charging up like a reusable battery. I walked around the psych ward with my headphones on, feeling the chi of the songs, connecting my feet to Mother Earth. I was in heaven. My body felt light, my motion effortless. I got my hands on some crayons and started drawing healing soul art for other patients. I got a nice ego boost out of gaining a small cluster of psychotic disciples.

It was 2006, and word had gotten out that the Mayan calendar was going to end in 2012, perfect fodder for the characteristic apocalyptic paranoia floating about the hospital. Many of my disciples were interested in what I had to say about the end of the world. I took out my crayons and drew a large *2012* across the page in blue. Then, I turned the twos into fish symbols, explaining, "The Second Coming marks the new age of enlightenment." After drawing a smiley face inside the zero, I pointed to the one. "There's only one God, and it's you," I told them with a huge grin. "Then you'll know bliss," I jested, as I pointed to the smiley-faced zero. "Twenty twelve will simply mark a shift in your own consciousness," I assured them.

I was like a cosmic jester, playing games with words and symbols, talking about God but secretly knowing I was referring to myself. I would meditate with a huge tree in the smoking area, placing my hands up to it, crouching down into my stance, and exchanging energy with the tree. I asked the tree for its healing energy and wisdom, and I could feel its gratitude for my acknowledgment. The other patients thought it was hilarious, and I knew that their enjoyment was just an extension of my vibration. They were absorbing my bliss.

There was one guy admitted a couple of days after I was, and I noticed him immediately. He looked to me to be as bright as the sun. He came outside to the courtyard where everyone was smoking. He was wearing bold black sunglasses and a bright orange shirt, and his hair was spiked up with gel. His aura was pure gold.

I walked right up to him and asked, "Do you practice energy healing?"

He was totally shocked. "Yeah, man, I get energy work done. Why'd you ask me that?"

He was pretty freaked out. I told him that his energy was just incredibly vibrant and clear. I wanted to know more about him. He told me he'd confided in his therapist that he was feeling suicidal, so his therapist had put him on a psychiatric hold, requiring that he be committed to the hospital for further evaluation. I was surprised to hear that he felt angry.

"I'm going to sue her the second I get out of here," he exclaimed.

In that moment, I realized that not all people with good energy were enlightened. For the first time, I thought that maybe I could be both sick and enlightened. Maybe the medicine could treat the paranoia yet allow me to retain my recent realization. There was only one way to find out, and since my attempts to convince the staff of my divinity were failing, I foresaw that at some point I'd have to take the medicine.

My favorite staff members were these two Jamaican guys; they delighted me to no end. I loved everything about them: their accents, their demeanor, their smiles, the way they talked to me. They were awesome.

I asked them, "Is it true Jamaicans believe Bob Marley was a prophet?"

One replied, "I don't believe he's a prophet; I *know* he's a prophet!"

I laughed and leaned toward them, onto the counter that separated the staff from the patients. "Let me tell you a secret: I'm a prophet just like Bob Marley."

I'd never seen two people crack up so fast in my life.

But the other one soon stopped laughing and asked me, "Boy, when ya gonna stop foolin' around and take ya meds?"

Even though I made it a little while without taking medication, it wasn't long before I was begging for something to make the paranoia stop. The nights continued to bring on terrible spirits that were trying to hurt me. Some construction workers happened to come into the building, and I started imagining they were there to take me out. There was one in particular, a big Hispanic man, whom I kept locking eyes with. I thought for sure he was there to kill me.

By the time I started taking medication, I was so worked up that it took about a week for me to come down. I kept seeing the construction worker everywhere. It never occurred to me that I was possibly freaking him out because I was always staring at him.

After a few days, I walked by him in the hallway, and he whispered kindly, "I'm praying for you." *What a gentle soul inside such a big man*, I briefly contemplated. His words were like a sword of truth, cutting right through my insanity. I could see my psychosis for the first time, even if just a glimpse.

I hoped to God that my newfound enlightenment was real, but I remembered from last time that my mystical feelings disappeared with psychiatric treatment. *They may be able to drug my body*, I told myself, *but they cannot medicate my soul.* I needed a miracle. If the medicine didn't relieve me of my enlightenment, then my revelations must be real. Otherwise, I was back in the same boat as last time.

I supposed there were two things going on: there was my enlightenment, which was beyond my body, and there was psychosis, which was the manifestation of my enlightenment in my body. I believed bipolar was the biological effect, whereas God was the spiritual cause, that my condition was the result of spiritual attunement in a body unfit for awakening. I started imagining that my new purpose was to help society tease out mental illness from spiritual realization. I needed to prepare the world for the age of enlightenment, for the prophesied reality of heaven on earth.

Maybe people needed psychiatric care, but without spiritual counsel from other enlightened souls, treatment would remain incomplete. If the medical community kept pathologizing spirituality, nothing would ever change, and without more enlightened beings, we were all going to burn in the hell of our own creation.

It all made perfect sense. That is, until the meds started working.

Chapter 28

LET ME OUT PATIENT

It was difficult to tell which hurt worse, the postmanic depression or the spiritual fall from grace. Both fed off each other as I plummeted into a pit of despair, struggling to accept that all I understood of God might be the function of faulty neurology. Nothing had ever felt more real in my life, and yet reality was calling, pressuring me to let go of my recent revelations. I must yield to this material truth that bipolar disorder, an immeasurable chemical chaos in my brain, was stoking my cognition, causing God to appear in places where I shouldn't be finding Him.

The thing about taking antipsychotic medications was that they took a while to work, but when they did, they seemed to work overtime. The Spirit was gone. I imagined that maybe I'd been possessed by an alien entity, that I'd been abducted somehow and then returned to my body at normal levels of consciousness. I wasn't enlightened. I wasn't even spiritual. I was just Chris again.

Then, as quickly as lucidity came back, fatigue took hold. I was exhausted, barely able to get out of bed. My mind was foggy, my cognition delayed. As foretold by the doctors, depression set in, the inevitable result of an overloaded nervous system high on mania.

Some things had changed in Ridgeview's outpatient program since I'd been there a few years ago. There was a dual-diagnosis track now, a tailored program for those patients fortunate enough to be both addicted to drugs and/or alcohol and also diagnosed with a mood disorder. They let me know that I was both bipolar and addicted to mood-altering substances, a more rare and yet often comorbid pairing of psychological dysfunction.

I certainly wasn't ready to stop drinking, and, as had been the case in other group-therapy settings, I didn't fully relate to the stories of other addicts and alcoholics. They would talk about drinking and drugging around the clock, about not being able to stop. I didn't feel that way. I partied hard, sure, but I also took care of myself. I was still productive most of the time, provided I wasn't manic or depressed. I got stoned only after I took care of my responsibilities. I tried to get wasted only on the weekends. I continued to guard myself against labels of addiction and alcoholism: "I'm just bipolar. This is just depression."

My feelings of denial translated to incessant complaints about the outpatient program to my parents. I told them it was a waste of my time. I explained all the ways in which I was different from the other patients. I appealed to their concerns that my level of care was less than exemplary. Desperate to get me help, my parents started looking up top treatment programs in the country, and they found one of the best in the world: Sierra Tucson, an expensive, internationally acclaimed treatment center in Tucson, Arizona. My parents told me about how Sierra Tucson had the best treatment available, how they had horse rides and yoga classes and world-class cooking. They even had biofeedback and energy healing and massage available to their clients. It sounded way better than Ridgeview, and so I agreed to go.

I shared with my therapy group about how I was leaving them for a better program, and they were appropriately skeptical. "Sounds like a vacation," they smugly replied. My group leader and case manager wished me luck, but he encouraged me to realize that no matter where I went, I was not going to recover until I started getting honest about my problems. He often spoke in aphorisms, saying, "No matter where you go, there you are." His wise words resonated, but I still wouldn't be able to hear them for quite some time.

Arizona was beautiful, but it didn't really matter because I was so sedated and depressed, coming off my manic high and dosed with what I reckoned was enough antipsychotic medication to stifle Jesus Himself. One of the program's escorts picked me up from the airport and took me to the facility, which looked like a mix between a dude ranch and a resort. Their posh, Western-style cabins were always full, and I was told a room would be made available to me once I showed full participation in the program. Until then, I would stay in their separate detoxification area, a small, sterile section of the main building resembling a hospital.

I must have slept three days straight once I got there, waking up only for exams and meals. I wasn't allowed to have coffee or diet soda, and that was the only way I'd been getting through any of my groups at Ridgeview, so the caffeine-free living hit me hard. I didn't bring any cigarettes either, so that was off the table. All my go-to stimulants were unavailable, and I was exhausted. The doctors started tinkering with my meds, hoping that I would perk up enough to join other clients in the various process groups.

Sierra Tucson had it all, but I was in such a state of confusion and hurt that I was hardly receptive. The best care in the world was at my fingertips, but none of it mattered. The more I learned of the treatment, the more hell-bent I was on getting out of there. I wasn't ready to work on myself. I believed my only problem was brain chemistry. The Sierra Tucson staff was pushing me to dig deep, to explore my pain and express my emotions. I wasn't ready, and I didn't think I'd ever be ready. My hurt seemed forbidden, almost radioactive, as if once touched, it might injure me beyond repair.

They gave me spiritual texts to contemplate, workbooks to complete, and all kinds of psychiatric evaluations. The conditions seemed ideal. If there was ever any hope of me getting help, if there was any chance of recovery, one would think that I might find it here, but so long as I refused, no amount of care would make a difference.

The group therapy sessions scared the hell out of me. They did all sorts of stuff Ridgeview didn't do. At one session, a fellow patient was instructed to talk to her sister by addressing an empty chair, the invisible representation of her family member's presence. Another patient was instructed to shout and hit an object with foam paddles to express his anger, for the rest of us to witness. It was all too bizarre for me. I was sure I would be doing no such things.

I took a few tests that evaluated my thoughts and behaviors to help diagnose my condition. The psychiatrist explained that they wanted to diagnose me themselves, that my bipolar diagnosis was uncertain due to my marked history of drug and alcohol abuse. He told me these tests would give them some clarity as to how to proceed. Sierra Tucson didn't assume anyone's medical history as fact, didn't accept anyone else's diagnoses. The clinicians took their own histories and conducted their own tests to determine necessary treatment.

When my results came back, they said that I didn't test very strong for bipolar disorder other than my psychotic episodes, but that I tested incredibly high for anxiety and addiction. I didn't like hearing that, especially not the part about addiction. I just wanted to be normal, and I couldn't imagine a normal life without at least some social drinking. Most of all, I didn't want to have a substance-abuse problem. They outlined my treatment plan, prescribing me with multiple daily groups for the treatment of alcoholism and addiction.

I didn't even make it out of their detox and evaluation unit before I convinced my parents to let me return home and complete Ridgeview's outpatient program instead. Sierra Tucson wasn't covered by our insurance; it was supposed to be a gift. My brief stay had already cost my parents thousands of dollars, so it wasn't very difficult to convince them that their money could be better spent. I told them Sierra Tucson was just a cushy, expensive version of Ridgeview, and I promised to take my treatment seriously upon my return.

I wasn't ready to give up alcohol, no matter what the costs. I couldn't live without drinking. My friends would disown me. I could never date again. My entire social life would disappear. My life would be over. I would've rather died than live sober.

I met with my assigned psychiatrist and told him that I appreciated his time and effort, but that I didn't need this level of care. I just needed to get my meds right and figure out how to return to my normal life. He encouraged me to stay, but said that he had no desire to keep someone against his or her will.

I returned to Atlanta, desperate to accept my bipolar treatment in order to keep my hopes of drinking alive. It felt good to be back at Ridgeview after Sierra Tucson; better the devil you know than the devil you don't. All those wacky therapy techniques had freaked me out. Back in the safety of Ridgeview, I put my head down, said the right things, and got my work done. I went to my meetings. I shared my thoughts when it was my turn to speak. I did what I had to do to get out. I served my time.

Chapter 29

THE BINGING BARISTA

It wasn't too long after I'd returned to living with my parents that we started brainstorming what I was going to do with my life. I didn't feel spiritual at all anymore. I felt incredibly jaded. There wasn't a God, and if there was, He definitely had no interest in helping me. My belief in enlightenment was shattered. Spirituality was nothing but a bunch of people engaged in a collective psychosis, convinced of their delusional belief in a greater power, unable to admit the futility of their faith and service. If they knew what I knew, they'd be depressed too.

Thanks to a note from my psychiatrist, I was allowed to finish my courses that I'd dropped at Life University. All I had left to finish the term were my final exams. I could barely think straight, let alone recall the complicated physics I had learned only a few weeks prior. I bombed the exam, but I still passed the course. I'd had an A+ before dropping out, but my final exam score left me with a C. School was clearly not going to be in the cards right now. I needed some time off. I needed to do something I had pretty much never done before: get a job.

As depressed and tired as I was, it felt impossible to even get out of bed, let alone get a job. My mom used her cheerleading skills to boost me into action, all but holding my hand through the door of Starbucks. She helped me complete a resume and cover letter, bought me new clothes to wear since I was already rapidly gaining weight, and drove me to various Starbucks locations to ask for work. Starbucks sounded like the perfect job: they had good benefits, were considered a great company, and could bolster my resume regardless of what I ultimately chose to do with my life.

I fought my mom on the whole thing. "They aren't hiring," I insisted. She had me go anyway and coached me on the proper steps. I would walk in; drop off my completed application, résumé, and cover letter; ask to speak with the manager; and then follow up with a phone call. It worked. About a week after going around to different stores and calling the managers, I was asked to come in for an interview.

Starbucks marked my quasi recovery, as I spent the next year living at home and healing from the detrimental effects of psychosis. At work, I would binge drink coffee products just to make it through my shift. When I got home, I'd binge eat leftover items marked out from the store, mainly loaves of pound cake and sandwiches. If I wasn't working, eating, or watching television, I was sleeping. I had never been more depressed in my life.

There was a shotgun rack in my parents' house, right behind the chair where I'd sit and watch television. Every time I'd come back from getting more food from the kitchen, my eyes would wander to the glass display. Suicidal for the first time in my life, I'd imagine scenarios in which I'd put the barrel in my mouth and pull the trigger. Before I went to sleep, I'd hope to die softly in the night. I didn't want anyone to feel the pain of my suicide, so I'd fantasize about a world where no one would miss me, and my death would cause no grief. I wished I had never been born.

I put on a good front for everyone. Except for my parents, no one seemed to detect how difficult a time I was having. At work, there were times when I would profusely sweat, consumed by the social anxiety of my job, but I would blame it on the hot coffee. I would have to take breaks in the walk-in fridge to cool off. Despite my inner agony, I still received high marks on my performance. I was on two different shifts that got perfect scores for customer-service excellence. Starbucks would hire secret shoppers to grade us on our jobs, and I always scored well.

Without God, life became increasingly dull and insignificant. I hardly believed in enlightenment or spiritual pursuits at all, equating God's existence with about the same probability that I actually was the Second Coming of Christ. I grew convinced that religion was a psychological phenomenon, and I chalked up all my rapidly dissolving spiritual insights to my mood disorder. I convinced myself that God was a function of neurosis, and served primarily to ease society's existential angst. There was no such thing as chakras; chi was just a psychosomatic phenomenon. Auras were hallucinations. Miwa and the rest of the Dahn masters were a bunch of brainwashed cult victims.

As far as exercise was concerned, I wasn't working out at all. I felt too tired. My depression and accompanying binge eating earned me another forty pounds or so of weight gain, and the idea of dieting and exercising all that weight off again felt impossible. I started searching for easier means of weight loss. I looked for dieting efforts that would be faster, more drastic, and require less prolonged dedication.

I came across a strategy called the "Master Cleanse" and began fasting. The Master Cleanse was a ten-day diet of lemon juice, cayenne pepper, and maple syrup. I read that you could go as long as you wanted on the cleanse, but that ten days was the suggested minimum to reap its benefits, mainly weight loss, detoxification, and renewed vitality. The morning ritual was a "salt-water flush," a liter of water combined with sea salt, meant to flush out toxins. I was determined to follow it, certain I could do anything for just ten days.

My preparation for the Master Cleanse was thorough. I went to the grocery to buy all the lemons, maple syrup, cayenne pepper, and sea salt I would need. The most important part of the pre-cleanse process, though, was the purchase of my last supper prior to the big starve. I planned to hit some fast-food drive-thrus, buy some ice cream and chocolate, and prepare for an evening of gorging myself into a near-catatonic state. I figured I might eat enough that I wouldn't even want food for the next ten days. I would emerge from my food coma the next morning full of just enough shame, guilt, and self-hatred that I'd be ready to take on my period of starvation. I planned a couple of days off work to coincide with the beginning of the fast, so I could just sleep all day.

The start was the salt-water flush. I would choke down the salt water and then, within an hour or so, begin hosing water out my ass. The first day, not much happened since I was so backed up. By the third day, the only thing coming out of my rectum was a yellowish liquid sprinkled with little red dots of ground-up cayenne pepper.

My parents were encouraged by my renewed motivation; dieting always had a way of putting pep in my step. The lemonade concoction began tasting really good to me after a while. I looked forward to the sweet and spicy drink. I would drink it at home and all throughout my shifts. Despite the misery of the first few days, I soon began feeling great. I was ecstatic to find myself losing over a pound a day. I bragged to my fellow baristas that I didn't even care to eat anymore. The Master Cleanse was doing incredible work on me. I couldn't believe I'd never heard of it before. By the end of the ten days, I had lost about fifteen pounds and felt energized for the first time since my hospitalization. I was determined to go on as long as I could.

Day eleven rolled around, and I began thinking that maybe I'd go forty days and forty nights, just like Jesus did. Maybe there was something spiritual happening to me throughout this whole fast after all. I now understood why religions used fasting. I felt in touch with my spirit for the first time since my supposed enlightenment, and my insight into the detoxification and purifying process of fasting led me to believe, once again, that God existed beyond biology, if accessible only in the heightened states of neurological disorganization. In this case, bodily starvation meant spiritual nourishment.

On day twelve, my parents went out of town for the weekend, and so I decided to have a party. So much for my spiritual realignment. I broke my twelve-day fast with a twelve-pack of Bud Light. After waking up the next day from my blackout, I began preparing for my next round of the Master Cleanse, convinced I could fare better this time around.

The second time, I lasted only a few days before throwing in the towel. My original twelve-day stretch would be the only time I'd ever be able to go that long, but that wouldn't stop me from trying. I decided I would just do it as much as I could. My dietary habits became consumed by the binge-fast cycle. I would fast, and then I would binge in preparation for another fast, and round and round it would go.

It didn't take me long to hear about water fasting, where I could just fast on water alone. I started bypassing the whole Master Cleanse ordeal; it was too much work. My water fasts quickly turned into coffee fasts. I would head to Starbucks early in the morning, down my four shots of espresso and drink iced coffee all throughout my shift. Then I would be so ravenous that I'd get some food from the shopping center I worked in and eat it in my car before hitting a drive-thru for a second meal on my way home. I had absolutely no idea that I was in the grips of an eating disorder. All I knew about eating disorders was that anorexics were dangerously thin and bulimics threw up their food.

Every time I fasted, no matter how much weight I lost, I would gain it back and more. I got to the heaviest weight I'd ever been in my life, but I kept telling myself that I was just one good, long fast away from reclaiming my desired physique. My depression and disordered eating fueled each other. I was morbidly ashamed of my body, and the more ashamed I was, the more I ate, and the more I ate, the more depressed I became. I would break out into a nervous sweat if I saw anyone I hadn't seen in a while. I felt absolutely disgusting, and I kept using drugs and alcohol to compensate for my social anxiety.

A significant amount of my therapy and psychiatry appointments were spent talking about my bodily insecurities and my inability to diet effectively. The weight gain was always just chalked up to depression. It was a symptom of bipolar disorder. My psychiatrist prescribed me a medication that prevented the absorption of fat in my body. I took the pill, and fat deposits would pass through my bowels. It was gross. I would basically poop oil. There were a few times that I farted and the oily substance slipped out of my butt and stained my pants. No matter what I tried, I kept gaining weight, but I still felt relief, regardless of how fleeting, with each new attempt at dieting.

Chapter 30

BOTTOM

In brief moments of interspersed sanity, I contemplated my life. With all the spiritual and psychological confusion of my psychoses, I decided that I wanted to return to the University of Georgia to study theology and psychology, hopefully in a way that would allow me to evaluate and critique their overlap. I wanted to explore spirituality as a psychological phenomenon, with the intention of validating God as the singular truth beyond the confines of the fallible human mind. I knew there was validity to my experiences, no matter how muddled by faulty neurology and egocentric delusion. If I could just establish that God existed at the edge of human consciousness, perhaps I might find some significance, a purpose to all this madness.

At this point, I hadn't been in class for over a year while I worked at Starbucks and lived with my parents. Mom and Dad agreed that it was time for me to return to school, and we all longed for the day that I might be inspired to live a better life. College promised the opportunity for me to pursue happiness and fulfillment, and while once upon a time majoring in religion and psychology might have seemed impractical, at least I still cared about something. Financial success was not really the objective anymore; we all prayed that I might discover enough peace and happiness just to stay sane and productive.

It wasn't hard to reenroll at UGA and transfer my Life University credits. My parents and I worked out the stipulations of my reenrollment and decided it would be best for me to attend a summer course. This would allow me to ease back into the academic setting after my yearlong hiatus. It was assumed, and I had come to believe it myself, that after all I had been through, I would be able to take my collegiate responsibilities more seriously. Life had thrown a few curveballs my way, and we hoped that I had matured from these experiences, at least enough to keep my head screwed on straight. I made the usual promises to myself: I'd go to class, hit the gym, confine my drinking to small amounts during appropriate times, and avoid drugs entirely.

I didn't last a week before I started skipping class. My social anxiety was at an all-time high. I couldn't stand being in my body. Even if I wanted to go to class, the summer heat, combined with my nervousness, ensured that I would sweat profusely throughout the entire lecture. It was the most uncomfortable I had ever been in my life. I was embarrassed to see anyone I knew, because they must either be judging my body, or wondering where I had been, or thinking about how I was a crazy person. I was allowed three missed classes, and I quickly used up all of them. I told myself, "Next week, I'll start going every day."

I had until Monday to party, and then I needed to get serious. I had said I wouldn't do drugs, but I bought some cocaine, thinking it might provide some confidence and help me lose weight. I figured if I just used a little bit at a time, no one would be able to tell I was stoned, and I could reap all the rewards without any side effects. I went out that weekend, but even drunk and high, I couldn't enjoy myself. I was too embarrassed. I felt like a total loser, and I didn't want to see anyone or talk about anything. Life had completely lost its luster, and no amount of intoxication could delude me into thinking I was anything short of a privileged piece of shit with no hope and zero direction.

I did so much coke that I convinced myself I was sober. I left the bars and headed for my car. When I sat down in the driver's seat and started the engine, I noticed a police car at the far end of the parking lot. In a split second, I decided that I was good enough to make it home without giving probable cause for them to pull me over. With a gram of cocaine in my pocket, and after a few hours of drinking, I pulled out of the lot, right in front of the cops, expecting them to just let me drive off without notice.

The moment I pulled past their vehicle, the police turned on their headlights and pulled out behind me. They started tailing my car so close that I couldn't even see their headlights. I quickly decided to drive to my nearest friend's apartment, which was only about a mile away. I drove exactly the speed limit and tried to stay as calm as possible. I began having imaginary conversations with the officers, trying to prepare myself for the inevitable dialogue, during which I would just hope to God they didn't find the cocaine in my pocket. I started thinking up ways I could ditch my stash, and I considered swallowing the bag whole.

After a few minutes, I turned into my buddy's complex, and for whatever reason, the officers kept on driving. My close escape from the police served as a wake-up call, as if I really needed one. I was out of control. I'd said I wouldn't do drugs, and here I was, less than a week in, putting myself in position to get a DUI and cocaine possession. As I snorted the remaining cocaine, I admitted to myself for the first time that there was no possible way for me to use drugs and alcohol moderately.

I spent the rest of the weekend lying low, drinking whiskey, eating fast food, and playing online poker. I had gotten into the habit of playing online poker while I lived at home with my parents, depositing twenty dollars at a time to play. It seemed harmless enough, but for whatever reason, this weekend, I thought it would be fun to try online blackjack. I got up about a thousand dollars and was thrilled, and then I immediately lost it all and spent every dime in my bank account trying to get it back. So now, I was broke. The only money I had left was the cash in my wallet.

Monday arrived, and I slept through my class. I had officially missed too many classes to pass, and so I dropped my only summer course. I lied to my parents and friends, and pretended to continue to go, but I knew it was just a matter of time before I had to come clean. I had enough money to last me about a week. The jig was up, but even then, I didn't stop drinking.

I continued considering the inconvenient truth, that I was truly an alcoholic and drug addict, and I had no choice but to finally get help. I needed to stop blaming bipolar disorder for my substance abuse. The whispers of my conscience had grown into screams. All the mood swings and psychotic episodes, were they not directly related to my substance abuse? What was mania besides the break from feelings of nervousness and agitation following one of my binges or weeklong benders? I finally knew what needed to be done. I had to go to rehab. *I'm not bipolar. I'm an alcoholic. I'm an addict.*

On my last night in Athens, I was so emotional that I couldn't sleep. With no alcohol or money, I was terrified to approach my parents with more devastation. I spent the majority of the night weeping, praying to God to please save my life, confessing that I was totally out of control and needed His help and guidance. I pleaded for a return to the loving and responsible person I once was before drugs and alcohol took me out. I promised God that if He would only grant me new life, I would be a living testament of His grace.

In no specific sensation, I began to feel His presence. There was a ray of light amid the darkness, a sense of hope that all was not lost. It was not too late for me to be saved, and though I couldn't describe what was happening, I knew that God was entering me in a new and profound way. For the first time, I could see clearly that my lack of humility was the source of my spiritual confusion. God was constant, and it was I who had been flickering in and out of existence, not Him. I kneeled on the ground next to my bed, tears streaming down my face, and with every ounce of sincerity I had to offer, I muttered a familiar prayer: "Lord, I am not worthy to receive You, but just say the word and I shall be healed."

Part Three

REVELATION

Chapter 31

THE EXPERIMENT

My bipolar disorder and addiction were so symbiotic that it was impossible for me to comprehend one without the other. Prolonged substance abuse preceded my every manic episode. Every morning after a drinking binge, I would wake up feeling irritable and anxious until I could either drink more or sleep it off. My major psychotic episodes followed many days of drinking, drug use, and sleep deprivation. I knew that while I might be bipolar, I couldn't know for sure unless I was sober. I decided to undergo the ultimate experiment: stop using drugs and alcohol, discontinue all medication, and see what happened.

I told my parents everything. I confessed how I'd gambled all my money away, how I couldn't come up with rent, how I'd withdrawn from school, and how I was finally ready to get sober. They were immediately concerned that I was manic. I was emphatic that they needed to trust me, that my substance use was out of control, that it had been for some time now, and that it wasn't just a symptom of bipolar. They were terrified to hear that I wasn't taking my medication, so I agreed to see my psychiatrist right away.

When we got to Dr. Layne's office, he was quick to try to deter me from my plan. He agreed that I needed to stop drinking and using drugs, but he was mainly concerned with regulating my mood. I told him what I had already told my parents, that I didn't want to take medication for bipolar disorder until I had been sober for some time. I explained that I viewed all of my bipolar symptoms as coinciding with my substance abuse and withdrawal, and I felt like I would never know for sure that I was bipolar until I experienced mood disturbances while sober.

He disagreed: "If you don't take medication, I guarantee you'll need hospitalization within ninety days."

I crossed my arms. "Well then, at least I'll know for sure."

My parents were there for the whole thing, and they were frightened at the prospect of another psychotic episode. Dr. Layne's alarming prognosis put us all on edge.

When we got home, they threatened to kick me out of the house: "If you're not going to work with us on your treatment, Chris, you'll have to find somewhere else to live."

"I'd rather be homeless than take meds," I told them. "The medicine is terrible. It makes me gain weight. It totally changes my personality."

I insisted that I needed treatment for substance abuse and addiction. I swore up and down that I knew my mind, that I wasn't going manic. "I just need rehab. You have to trust me! I've never been compliant. I've lied to Dr. Layne for years. I'm not bipolar. I'm an alcoholic. I've never had a problem sober. Bipolar people can't go this long without medication. Let me prove it to you, please."

Mom and Dad eventually agreed to allow me to continue without medication, provided that we monitor my mood and sleep, and if my behavior started to change, I would be willing to take something.

After a few days of sleeping and maintaining sobriety, I started to level out, and my parents became much more receptive to the idea of sending me to rehab. Some more lucid conversations helped ease their anxiety around Dr. Layne's scary prediction. I explained how dishonest I had been. I confessed that I had always been resistant to sobriety, but that in my heart, I just knew it was the key to my health. After learning the extent of my deceit, they agreed to send me to rehab for alcohol and drugs, provided that I stay open to my bipolar diagnosis.

A friend of my parents recommended a recovery program in Utah called Wilderness Quest. I had heard of wilderness rehab programs before, and since I'd felt such a major shift during my time at the National Outdoor Leadership School, I figured this type of setting would be perfect.

I would be outside, connecting to nature, free from distraction and temptation. I would get plenty of exercise and hopefully lose a lot of weight. I'd never felt better than after my thirty-day wilderness expedition, so if I could combine that experience with drug and alcohol rehabilitation, I figured I'd be primed for a successful recovery.

The only problem was, when we contacted the program, their medical staff said that my BMI was way too high. They were concerned about my ability to endure the daily hikes. They wanted me to lose some weight, and then I could go. It was time for another diet.

I looked up the latest diet craze and discovered the alkaline diet, which required eating foods with a specific pH effect on the body. It was supposed to promote detoxification and weight loss. Basically, meat, dairy, and sugar were all off-limits. Nearly every green plant was very good as far as alkalinity. It was a highly plant-based diet, and I was supposed to eat as much raw plant material as possible, since cooking somehow diminished the nutritional value of the food.

At this point, it didn't matter what I was eating; I overate. The diet was very hard for me to follow, not surprisingly. It had been over a year since I could successfully follow a diet. I spent about a month trying to lose weight, and after my dieting yielded little to no results, Wilderness Quest said I could come, provided I get proper medical authorization. After I passed some general cardiovascular and endurance tests, and once my blood work checked out, we booked me a one-way ticket out West. A mixture of hope and terror enlivened my soul as I considered the possibility of my return to health.

Off I went on a flight to Utah, armed only with my copy of *The Power of Now* and the sincere willingness to be remade. I felt connected to a higher reality, and even though I wasn't readily calling my spiritual connection "God," I knew that there was some benevolent energy in my favor. By my estimation, it was a miracle that I was even still alive, let alone in such a fortunate position to get help. If I hadn't been born into such privilege, I would undoubtedly be homeless or in prison. I could feel a sense of purpose, and I knew that I was embarking on a journey that would drastically alter the outcome of my life. I was ready to be healed, once and for all.

Two Wilderness Quest employees picked me up from the airport. To my surprise, one of them was only a year older than I was. He told me that he'd gone through the program himself before coming back to work there. He seemed genuinely happy. After a long drive, we arrived at base camp, a small cluster of buildings on the edge of the tiny town of Monticello, Utah. The staff outfitted me with all the gear and clothing I would need for my time in the woods. They said the average stay was forty-five days, but I wouldn't know for sure until I did all the work needed to graduate. I was driven out to meet my group, ready for my month and a half without a warm shower, fresh clothes, or cushy bed.

They gave me a journal, a workbook, and a couple of twelve-step books. Reading the recovery literature assured me that I was making the right decision to get sober. I related to everything in the books. I was definitely alcoholic, and I desperately wanted to believe that a Higher Power was strong enough to heal me of this painful affliction. I was sure that I'd encountered some sort of spiritual power, but whether that energy could work in my favor was an entirely different question.

I met the other students, and we began doing our group sessions and therapeutic check-ins. We would discuss how we were doing emotionally, mentally, physically, and spiritually. We were instructed to tell one another our life stories and share completed assignments in which we recounted our destructive behaviors. I talked a lot about struggling with whether or not I was bipolar and, in addition, whether or not I needed medication. I continued to believe that if I stayed sober and clean, I wouldn't have such a difficult time controlling my emotions.

Wilderness Quest offered the perfect balance of therapy and wilderness training. I felt pushed but not overwhelmed. I was assigned a therapist, whom I met once a week, and between those visits, two or three field instructors accompanied us, depending on the group size. Staff led groups and taught us wilderness skills, reporting our progress to the clinicians. During any downtime, I was encouraged to journal, complete workbook assignments, or practice making a fire from sticks, and various other survival skills.

There was a considerable detoxification effort still taking place, even though I had already been sober for a couple of months. I was exhausted for the first few weeks. I wasn't drinking caffeine, eating refined sugar, or using tobacco products. Then, right about when I couldn't stand any more melancholy, I started feeling better, a lot better. I was loving life—hiking all day, learning wilderness survival skills, and authentically discussing my emotions, without reservation, for the first time in my life. My confidence was growing, and I started really believing I could live a life of permanent recovery from mood-altering substances.

The staff made it clear that I had to go all in on recovery, or else I wasn't going to stay sober. I believed them. I tried not to hold anything back. I discussed old heartbreak and confusion, and it seemed like every therapeutic assignment yielded greater and deeper realization of buried pain. For the first time ever, I started acknowledging my social anxiety and body shame. Even though it had been years, I found myself writing feverishly in my journal about my unrequited love for Chloe, and how hard it was to let go of what I was certain was true love. I even talked about my difficulty with God and spirituality. I had to get over old ideas of masculinity and embrace the power of vulnerability. I had no choice but to get real, and contrary to my conditioning, I felt stronger, not weaker, as the result.

There were a couple of staff members in recovery themselves, and they inspired me to want to go further. My every thought became dedicated to recovery. It was as if I were addicted to everything in my life: drugs, alcohol, food, sex, even love. This all made sense when I looked through the lens of spiritual suffering. If the source of my suffering was spiritual, then there was no physical means of satisfying it. My spiritual malady, the "hole in my soul," could be filled only by a power greater than myself. I had to learn how to access my Higher Power, and I could see that the smaller I became, the more humble I made myself, the less ego and attachment I had, the more complete I felt. The promise of salvation was as real as ever.

One of the staff introduced me to Jungian dream analysis, and I started using the ideas to examine my psychotic episodes. I had always felt like I was in a waking dream during my times of delusion, and Carl Jung's methods of interpreting symbols, metaphors, and archetypes astounded me. It was like learning the language of my mind, unlocking layers of vaulted confusion and freeing endless creativity. Perhaps Jesus represented my psyche's ideal, a drive to be perfect in the eyes of God, some primordial desire to die and be reborn, a calling to be the savior of my own life. Maybe my perfectionism was what needed crucifying. I started looking at everything through the lens of psychological metaphor and imagery. There was no limit to life's symbolism. Psychosis was like the spiritual coup d'état of my unconscious mind. Life itself became a dream, a series of signposts endlessly pointing me back to Spirit.

I started having strange encounters with my mind, in which I knew there was an underlying wisdom, perhaps my soul, guiding my discoveries. I would see a wild animal and feel as if its presence was communicating a message to me, supporting me in my efforts. I would have a conversation with another student and sense that there was a hidden meaning in his words. Even the wind felt like a spiritual embrace, a message from God that He was still with me. My every thought turned to spiritual connection with God and the oneness of nature. I wondered if I was becoming psychotic, but the staff assured me that my sleep, my mood, my behavior were normal. There was nothing wrong with being a spiritual person.

Even though I had processed quite a lot of emotion during my time at Wilderness Quest, I still hadn't cried. Then one day, while we were climbing a steep rock face, I got so scared that I couldn't move my body at all. Paralyzed with fear, I broke down and began to weep. My mind was like a dam collapsing, and the raging waters, years of suppressed emotions, flooded my entire being. The experience felt like a sort of baptism, washing my soul clean. I was once again in touch with my sensitive nature, that part of me that I never allowed expression, and I knew that it was from this place that I needed to rebuild my life.

All of my suffering, all the pain and anguish, was exactly what I needed to get me to this point. I was finally free. I could feel the emergence of the divine feminine within, and I began to embody an authentic masculinity. My previous identity crises were the unraveling of fragile ego structures, a soul wisdom desperate to reveal my highest nature in union with God. By the end of my program, I had never felt saner or more comfortable in my skin, and it had been over ninety days since Dr. Layne promised me that I would go psychotic without medication. I passed the test, and my faith was restored. I didn't need to be hospitalized. I didn't need medication. All I needed to do was stay sober and trust in God. The rest would work itself out.

Chapter 32

REAL LIFE

Upon my graduation from Wilderness Quest, my therapist recommended, and my parents agreed, that I enroll in a transitional living program in Boulder, Colorado, called AIM House ("Where Actions and Intentions Merge"). The benefits of a sober living environment were numerous. The most important asset, as far as I could tell, was that I wouldn't be returning home. I had changed a lot in a very short period. Previously, anytime that I'd felt close to improving my life, I would spoil my efforts by throwing myself right back into the same situations as before. A fresh start in a new environment would be critical to my long-term success.

Before I left for Colorado, I received the best advice I'd ever heard. My therapist told me, "Don't ever forget: every choice is a matter of 'hard-easy' or 'easy-hard.' You can either do the hard work now, and it will be easier later on, or you can take the easy way out and pay for it later." "Hard-easy" became my recovery mantra, where I would welcome challenge and embrace fear, trusting that God was giving me exactly what I needed for my growth, no more than I could handle, but certainly no less either.

I hoped that my bipolar episodes were behind me now that I was no longer abusing drugs and alcohol. I was absolutely dedicated to my sobriety, willing to do whatever it took, to live wherever I needed to live, and to give up whatever relationships I needed to in order to maintain my recovery. Bipolar disorder became a distant second in my concerns, but to be safe, I would continue psychiatric evaluations.

While my dedication to my sobriety never wavered, after only a week of being at AIM House, I started getting sour on the whole deal. It seemed like none of my peers actually wanted to be there, let alone stay sober. I couldn't really blame them, since I'd been in the same boat before, but this was way different from what I'd expected. It was rare for any of the other guys in the house to choose to go to recovery meetings or even take the therapy groups seriously. They seemed to participate only when it was required, and even then, they did the bare minimum. Our group sessions consisted primarily of a bunch of whining. I called home to my parents: "This is not what I signed up for. I'm living with a bunch of brats. None of them even want to be here."

Beyond my distain for my fellow inhabitants, I had major problems with the way the program worked, and initially, this was all around diet and exercise. The meals weren't healthy enough. There weren't daily trips to the gym. I wasn't getting enough exercise, and I couldn't diet. My plan to lose weight was already failing. I complained about the food incessantly. Something as simple as a sandwich was an abomination, a threat to my survival. I started insisting that I have a place to store separate groceries.

My entitlement really started to show. I had my parents strong-arm the program into letting me go on a family vacation. I bypassed the allowance system by getting my parents to send me a credit card, insisting that I needed the extra funds to support healthy eating habits. My therapist confronted me about how demanding I was with the program, other participants, and my parents. She questioned my sincerity in getting better if I was so unwilling to compromise around finances and house rules. I tried to change therapists, citing that I didn't want a therapist who didn't believe in me, but the treatment team required me to stay with her. I even considered leaving, but my parents wouldn't let me.

I eventually found a way to make it work. I wasn't going to be able to manipulate my way out of this one, and in my heart, I really did want to get better. I leaned into the hard-easy wisdom imparted on me, and even though it was difficult, I started getting honest and willing to hear the truth. I had thought that simply removing drugs and alcohol would fix me, but there was much more work ahead. The more grounded I got in recovery and the longer I stayed sober, the more realistic my expectations became. Most people naturally learn to deal with anxiety and insecurity, but my development had been thwarted by years of substance abuse. I didn't realize how much maturing I had to do, and there were some tough growing pains as I learned to stay with my thoughts and emotions over a longer period of time.

Even though I was struggling in a lot of ways, staying sober wasn't all that difficult in my new environment. I simply wasn't allowed to drink or drug. I could see it being harder if I was back home, and I found comfort in the rules and security of the house. My confidence in my sobriety also provided a pretty big ego boost. I was finally being good. More and more, I started shifting my focus to my sobriety, loosening my grip on "health" efforts of diet and exercise. I told myself I'd do sober now, and then I could get "healthy" later.

A month or two went by, and without alcohol or drugs, I started leaning on my more benign vices. I started using tobacco again, smoking cigarettes and dipping constantly. I'd drink entirely too much coffee in the morning and then supplement throughout the day with Diet Coke. I bought ice cream and other snacks, taking my treats up to my room and eating them either by myself or in front of the television. My weight started going up fast. I was constantly in therapy, and it felt impossible to engage in such frequent emotional processing without soothing myself with food.

I was still very interested in spiritual and psychological thought, and as time went on, I started considering a career as a mental-health professional of some kind. As part of my progression in the program, it came time for me to dedicate a certain amount of hours to either working or going to school. I heard about a small liberal arts college called Naropa University, where many of the staff members attended graduate training in psychotherapy. Naropa offered an undergraduate degree in "contemplative psychology," combining courses in both Western and Buddhist psychology. Upon further investigation, I decided to apply.

My confidence had seriously waned since high school. I was a long way from my honor society days; much closer to my mind were my failings at UGA. I agreed with my treatment team and parents to just give it a shot, understanding that I could take it slow and see how it went. I wrote my application essay on *The Power of Now*, and how secular spirituality had positively affected my life and recovery. In my interview, I spoke to the admissions counselor about my substance-abuse history and how it explained my weak transferring grades from UGA. With the help of my high-school transcripts and a recommendation from one of my clinicians, I was accepted. Even though I was attending a Buddhist university, my parents were supportive. Mom's only request was "Chris, just please don't become a Buddha."

In the spring of 2008, I enrolled part-time. I was studying Western psychology in one class and Buddhist psychology in the other. A thought-provoking and inspiring combination, the two courses helped shape my early recovery as I considered each piece of material and attempted to apply the wisdom to my own life. For example, when I learned about B.F. Skinner and behaviorism in my Western psychology course, I considered how much of my emotional suppression was conditioned, a part of gender conformity. I started to examine how much of a role masculine ideals played in my denial. If I could view emotional expression as strength rather than weakness, I might rewire some old harmful programming.

Naropa's contemplative education approach involved a lot of self-reflection, and meditation was part of the curriculum. Students were encouraged to relate to the material on a personal level through our writing and oral assignments. One of the primary teachings of Chögyam Trungpa Rinpoche, the school's founder, was to be a spiritual "warrior" in the world. He said, "Real fearlessness is the product of tenderness. It comes from letting the world tickle your heart, your raw and beautiful heart. You are willing to open up, without resistance or shyness, and face the world. You are willing to share your heart with others." His teachings resonated immensely and provided great inspiration, fueling my recovery and helping me reframe my sensitive nature.

With all the therapy, recovery meetings, and AIM House commitments, my part-time school status rounded out a pretty busy schedule. I was doing really well in my classes, even though I still had a lot of social anxiety. I was afraid to talk too much to other students, and the intimate classroom settings of the small university made it difficult to avoid interaction. I feared my classmates might find out I was in a treatment program. I also noticed a great deal of performance anxiety around my schoolwork. I would painfully procrastinate on all of my assignments, but I stayed committed.

My attendance at Naropa University continued to complement my recovery in profound ways, so much that it was hard to attribute my healing to any one source. My education helped cultivate my understanding of the inner workings of the mind, deepened and developed my spiritual relationship with a Higher Power, and even allowed me to make connections between my Christian upbringing and Buddhist psychology. As I learned more about Buddhist principles, like compassion and egolessness, I couldn't help but think of Jesus. Life was all coming together, and the synchronicity was nothing short of magical. I could see an underlying unity to the world religions, and it alleviated much of my confusion. My contemplative education was bringing me closer to God, allowing for insight and understanding to take root where there had previously been only fixed ideas and rigid beliefs.

Most inspiring was that my bipolar condition seemed entirely nonexistent. By the end of the semester, I had been sober for nearly a year and still showed no sign of bipolar disorder. I continued to discuss my mood with my psychiatrist, but over time, everyone began doubting the severity and accuracy of my diagnosis. I just didn't display anything outside the norm for a recovering addict and alcoholic. The possibility was presented that for me, substance abuse could induce psychosis. I had long considered the correlation between my drug and alcohol use and my psychotic episodes, so it wasn't hard to get on board with this theory. The more time passed, the more confident I was in my sanity.

Recovery wasn't perfect, but I was finally getting used to being sober and could honestly imagine a life without drugs or alcohol. At this point, there was no mention of disordered eating, but that all changed when I asked my parents to send some old pictures of me with my shirt off as motivation to lose weight. When I shared them with my therapist, she recommended that I meet with an eating-disorder specialist. She said that the specialist might be able to help me gain proper perspective on nutrition and exercise. All I really heard was that I'd be meeting with someone to help me lose weight.

AIM House had a women's program in addition to the men's house, though we didn't interact with the women at all. We just knew they were in town; the staff did their best to keep the male and female programs entirely separate. Eating disorders and body-image concerns were generally considered female-specific problems, so Lisa, the eating-disorder specialist, worked exclusively with the women's house. It was a rare exception that her services were ever utilized for the men. Throughout my years of therapy and treatment for bipolar disorder and addiction, no one had ever mentioned disordered eating, not even once.

It took me only about half of my initial session with Lisa to realize I wasn't ready to seriously work on my eating and body-image issues. I felt as if I'd been ambushed. All she did was ask me a series of questions, but her approach felt aggressive to my unprepared psyche. Her examination of my family, my upbringing, my relationship to food and appearance—it was all too much. She asked about my father's profession and was extraordinarily intrigued to hear he was a plastic surgeon. She asked how young I was when I'd first started dieting, and I couldn't even recall a time when I hadn't been on a diet. I even confessed my diet pill addiction. I'd never felt more vulnerable in my life. Lightbulbs started going off in my head, as old traumas were uncovered and shaky belief systems challenged.

I could tell she knew my pain, but as much as I wanted to heal, I didn't have enough tools yet to face this piece of my story. I told her that I didn't feel ready to talk about the stuff she was bringing up, and she respected my boundaries, but not before encouraging me to be brave and continue exploring these issues. We decided I would continue to focus on my recovery from drugs and alcohol, but that she would make herself available if I wanted to meet more.

I didn't reach out to her for the rest of my stay at AIM House, but the seed of truth was already planted, and if recovery had taught me anything, it was that I couldn't unlearn the truth. No matter how much I tried to forget, the idea that I suffered from disordered eating was established.

Even without touching my body fixation and eating issues, there was plenty of work to be done. I was learning to tolerate the nasty parts of life, of others, of my own mind. The emergence of an inclusive worldview fused with every part of my life, and I practiced a more spacious disposition. A more open philosophy made room for the ability to love my neighbor, tap into my basic goodness, and generally see the suffering and beauty in all people. Recovery was softening my ego, that aspect of my psyche constantly making up rules and taking all-or-nothing approaches to life. I was learning to forgive myself, and by doing so, I felt more connected to others than ever before. I could see that my rigid thinking, this black-and-white, dichotomous mess of a mind, was entirely responsible for my pain. I had found my path.

Chapter 33

TOUCH AND GO

The semester was coming to a close, and I needed something to do for the summer. My parents and I, along with my treatment team at AIM House, began devising a plan for my transition out of the house. When I'd left Wilderness Quest, the director had told me he would be honored if I would return to the program as an instructor one day. He was proud of the work I'd done and said I should use my experience to help others. I'd greatly admired the staff at Wilderness Quest during my time there, and I could only hope to have the kind of impact on another student in the way they had influenced me. When I reached out to them, I was thrilled to get hired on for the summer season.

With nearly a year of sobriety under my belt, I left AIM House to return to where the whole party got started. I was equally excited to have the opportunity to lose weight as I was to help others get clean and sober. A whole summer in the woods would no doubt leave me in great shape, and it couldn't come at a better time, since upon my return to Boulder, I was going to enroll as a full-time student and live on my own. In other words, I could date again. The idea of dating, especially sober, scared me nearly to death, so I needed to at least look the part. I began to comprehend how intertwined my body obsession was with my sexuality, but I tried my best just to put the next foot forward and take things one day at a time. "Let go, and let God."

Being an instructor at Wilderness Quest brought new meaning to the phrase "fake it until you make it." I wanted to help these kids, but I was still in the midst of helping myself. Regardless, when I'd first ventured into recovery, a year of sobriety seemed impossible, so I knew that no matter where I was in my own recovery, I could still offer a great deal of hope and wisdom to those just beginning to imagine a life without drugs and alcohol. I tried my best to simply be honest. My transition to sober living had happened recently, so I was able to answer a lot of questions about what to expect.

I found myself talking a great deal about dangerous societal expectations surrounding masculinity and the emotional stoicism that so often prevented young men from reaching out for help and accepting treatment. I was mostly just regurgitating what I'd learned in school. I was a few years older than most of the kids I worked with, and I talked about how my own recovery had been stymied for years as the result of my refusal to explore my emotions. Every boy there could relate.

Speaking about the difficulties and triumphs of early sobriety helped me more than it possibly could have been helping the students. I grew more confident in how far I had already come. My recovery didn't need to be perfect. I could help others and still help myself.

It wasn't all good, despite my wishing to be fully healed. Being a wilderness instructor played nicely into my restriction-binge cycle of disordered eating behavior. I'd go into the woods for eight days and then be off for six days, and sometimes I'd even work a double shift. On my off-shifts, I'd smoke, chew, drink coffee, and "cheat eat." The first couple of days of each shift would be spent in misery as I withdrew from nicotine, caffeine, and sugar. Regardless, with all the hiking I did that summer, it wasn't hard to lose about thirty pounds. I knew my behavior was erratic, but so what if it was a little touch and go? I was making good progress, and I was still sober. Recovery was a spectrum, and I was well on my way toward health.

When the summer came to an end, my path was clear. I had finally found my vocation. Helping others find the strength and courage to be honest about their emotional life, especially the adolescents and young men, brought me closer to my true self, my soul-nature, the part of me that existed long before I learned how to suppress and hide. My ability to lead others into that forbidden terrain was my highest calling. God had sent me to earth in order to heal and be healed. I could see the purpose to my suffering. The psychoses, the addictions, the overidentification with my bodily form—these were my ways of refusing God's call. My soul had known all along. It was time to go back to Boulder to finish my degree and embrace a lifetime of service, so I could help others find their true identity in the great ineffable Spirit.

Life started picking up, and it wasn't long before I forgot I'd ever been sick. It was pretty obvious by now that my identity and sense of self had not been too solid. I had pledged a fraternity, joined a cult, and confused myself with Jesus, the Buddha, and Bob Marley. I'd gone from being an uptight conservative to a free-spirited liberal in a matter of a year. My growing momentum toward a profession in psychotherapy was something I clung to with full force. In the back of my mind, I just hoped I was right.

The clarity and confidence that accompanied sobriety cannot be overstated. What began as subtle increases in my ability to hold my head up and look people in the eye grew into an absolute conviction that I was living a life of integrity. I might have been taking the edge off with my disordered eating behavior, but for the most part, I had no escape, and I was proud to be living life on the real. I was forced to proceed fully awake, conscious of my thoughts and behaviors. I couldn't pass out. I couldn't get drunk or high. I had to stay with the moment.

Though I'd been in therapy for years, I'd always lied, and the level of honesty I was now exhibiting provided great healing. I was able to talk about my body-image insecurities, fears of intimate relationships, and hopes for a full return to health. I was able to admit to all the anger I'd built up about my upbringing, my long-held belief that I had to be perfect, and the pain I kept hidden from my parents. I started understanding emotional triggers. I could see how some conversations, personalities, and situations made me upset. I could see how judgmental comments stoked unhealed areas of my mind and touched on trauma from the past. I wished so badly for people just to live and let live without harming one another.

I was still socially anxious, but I wasn't letting it stop me from showing up any longer. I'd talk in class, even though I would get red with embarrassment. Messages about overcoming fear and anxiety resonated with me. I'd hear spiritual teachings at school and seek out books on spiritual awakening, only to find that many of the lessons were examining ways of overcoming fear and insecurity. I could see that spirituality and psychology went hand in hand.

I became a sort of gender rebel. "Real men acknowledge their emotions," I'd affirm to myself. I would intentionally break out of the gender straightjacket anytime I could. My Naropa education made it impossible for me to continue with the macho charade, and I actively sought out feminist thought, looking to many of my classmates and instructors for greater understanding of gender and sexuality. I came to understand the inherent, insidious cultural and personal pain presented in pornography, and though it was very difficult, I quit watching videos entirely. I even got a tattoo sleeve of the Immaculate Heart of Mary, my symbolic dedication to the divine mother, Jung's anima.

One day, as our social psychology class discussed the influence of nature and nurture on gender roles, my classmate Tyra insisted, "Chris, you're *queer*. You just don't know it."

"But I'm straight," I cautiously replied.

"You can be straight and still be queer. Queer just means you don't identify with traditional gender roles."

"Okay then," I bashfully chuckled. "I guess I'm queer!"

The remaining sexual shame, remnants from my early adolescent same-sex activity, was nearly obliterated by a little further education. Thank God for the psychological sciences. I was briefly introduced to the work of Alfred Kinsey, whose famous Kinsey Scale basically suggested that all people fall somewhere on a bisexual continuum, regardless of their heterosexual or homosexual leanings. The Kinsey Reports somehow affirmed what I had privately come to believe: that I was indeed a straight, somewhat bisexual man, and now, kind of queer too.

Life was changing fast, and I liked my newfound identity, however muddled it might have remained. The truth was, though, I didn't really need to claim any identity. My time at Naropa also taught me something about my privileged position. I was a wealthy, white, straight, Christian male. Nobody was going to knock down my door and demand that I declare myself. At this point in my journey, I was on fire, free as I'd ever been, and part of me wished someone would come knocking, so I could educate them on equality and responsibility and love.

I was genuinely learning to navigate this foreign and inspiring liberal terrain, questioning how to be an advocate and reduce discrimination and stigma in the world, and I'd often muse: *Where does mental health fit into all of this? At some point, are not all bigots, murderers, and rapists mentally ill? Were monsters like Hitler and bin Laden not victims of a loveless system? When people fail to see their interconnectedness to all of life, to their fellows and the planet, are they not divorced from reality? If disorder is a deviation from the norm, what happens when society falls victim to collective delusion?*

There were hardly ever any easy answers, but I was relaxing into a compassionate worldview that was nothing short of spiritual. Simply by comprehending the nature of suffering, I could feel Christ's forgiveness and Buddha's awakened heart. I was falling in love with a path of inter-spiritual contemplation. My heart was breaking, revealing its invincibility. I finally knew God.

As far as my recovery was concerned, I did everything I was supposed to do. I went to my meetings and participated whenever I could. Almost all of my friends were sober, and I really felt like I had found my people, my tribe. We weren't afraid to show emotion, to joke around, to discuss our past. It was like a breath of fresh air to be around so many young people trying to better themselves, emotionally and spiritually. I was home.

I was sober for almost another year and received many blessings from health professionals to pursue further healing without medication for bipolar, so I believed any concerns were behind me. The only thing missing was a girl. It was recommended that I not engage in sexual relations for the first year of sobriety, and I was more than happy to heed that advice since I was still working through unresolved feelings of sexual insecurity and shame. Ideas that I should wait until marriage for sex remained, and I still questioned whether I could satisfy a woman. Though I hinted at some of my issues, I kept my disclosure really general with my therapist. I talked about feeling like I wasn't attractive, wanting to lose weight, and my desire to be more disciplined with my exercise routine. Even then, I was relieved to hear from her that all women are not obsessed with appearance the way I was imagining.

My focus turned to dating, since this seemed to be my last hurdle. I was thriving in all other aspects as far as I was concerned. My first relationship was with a girl in recovery from alcoholism, and though we dated for only a few months, our time together was enough to help me gain confidence. All those relationship anxieties were not as big a deal as I had imagined. I used the spiritual insights I'd gained in school to help me move into the fear and act anyway. I was empowered by my ability to put myself out there, to be willing to get hurt. I was less afraid of being vulnerable.

When she broke things off, I was devastated, and I watched as my newly acquired confidence was shaken. She told me she wasn't looking for something as serious as I was, which of course made me question her sincerity, but I had to trust that a better relationship lay ahead. With a couple of years of sobriety under my belt, I stayed sober, and even though it was painful, the breakup didn't break me. It also helped that my school year was coming to an end. I was heading back to Utah for another summer at Wilderness Quest. Being of service to others had a way of helping me forget my problems.

Chapter 34

TRUE LOVE

Love was just an idea until I finally met her. She really was "the one," and I had never been more certain of anything in my life. There was nothing that I wanted more than to find my soul mate, the one God had chosen for me to spend the rest of my life with, to create a family with, to grow old with. I called home to my buddy Alex: "I'm not kidding, man. I'm going to marry this chick. If this doesn't work out, I'm becoming a priest!" There was an intuitive sense in my soul; the search was over.

Taylor and I met through a mutual friend and started chatting on Facebook while I was finishing up my second summer as a wilderness instructor. It was 2009, and I had been sober a little over two years. I was about to begin my senior year at Naropa University, and I had every intention of going to graduate school to become a clinical psychologist. The future was wide open. I believed that all my bipolar disorder woes were behind me, and I was surely healed from drug and alcohol addiction. After another summer in the woods, I was happy enough with my body, and so thoughts of disordered eating exited my mind. I had never felt healthier or more vibrant in my life. When I finished my last shift in the woods, I was excited to ask Taylor out, but I was also really apprehensive, since the hurt of my previous failed relationship was still pretty fresh.

It was love at first coffee date. Taylor wore a bright yellow blouse and tight blue jeans. She was gorgeous, a half inch taller than I was, standing at five eleven, with fair skin and the curves of a fifties pinup. Her long brown hair fell halfway down her back, and she had these big, piercing hazel eyes that turned green only when she cried, which she did when she told me how much she loved her family. She was twenty-eight, three years my senior. Here was a real woman.

She was private about her tattoos. They told a story of a fierce vulnerability, of a feminine feminist with hard-earned wisdom. My favorite was a gorgeous old-school half-sleeve on her left arm featuring a large brightly colored peacock—art from her early twenties as a "betty" in San Francisco. She'd grown up in Boston and then Colorado, and she had just moved back to Boulder from Palm Springs to be near her family. Her parents were both world-renowned scientists, but she was a mathematically challenged artist and had been for as long as she could remember, and so she sometimes felt like an outcast when really she was just wonderfully strange.

Taylor didn't care for sweetener in her latte, but she liked to sprinkle half a pack of raw sugar on top of the foam and watch the granules melt into puffy brown divots. She was adorably quirky. She carried around these big, square, baby-blue letter-pressed business cards with her information on one side and a cartoon sketch of a little girl and a dog and the phrase "diagonally parked in a parallel universe" on the other. She had a crazy little wiry-haired mutt whom she'd rescued from a kill shelter in southern California and named Lux, after her favorite character in *The Virgin Suicides*.

It felt so comfortable to talk to her, like we had known each other for eternity. Taylor had a warmth to her that was so genuine and refreshing. I couldn't get enough. I did most of the talking, which, of course, I liked. Falling for Taylor was an exercise in ultimate trust. *Please God*, I prayed, *let this be real.* We were on the same wavelength, firing on all cylinders. She was gorgeous, sober, loved Eckhart Tolle, and had already rejected all of my friends' advances. What else could a guy ask for?

Her artistic temperament must have been attracted to my hypomanic eccentricity. When we met, I was as enigmatic as ever, busy with school, using up all of my free time to read, write, meditate, and dream up new tattoos. I'll never forget quivering as I kissed her for the first time. It was so embarrassing, but typical of Taylor, she just rolled with it. She held me on the couch until I relaxed, playfully roasting me until I could get it together. She appreciated my sensitivity. If there was anything I could offer, it was an emotional presence, an ability to be real and the willingness to feel. Fireworks went off. We fell hard.

Taylor seemed stable in all the ways I wasn't. She was practical, levelheaded, and much more skeptical than I was. During one of our early philosophical musings, in which I was discussing the inherent divinity of all people, she jested, "What, do you think you're Jesus or something?" She didn't let me get away with anything; I'd met my match. She had my full attention, and I quickly became willing to give her my all.

Falling in love took me over, and it wasn't long before I noticed my mood was getting shaky. Our relationship became the sole focus of my mind, and the rest of life stopped coming so effortlessly. My concentration was off, and I found myself more easily irritated, as if my growing attachment to another person necessitated flares of intense agitation. I just assumed it was from staying up late with Taylor, cramming more on my assignments, and eating out more often on our dates. Eventually, I started openly obsessing about my sleep, diet, and exercise, since these were the three ways I tried my best to regulate my mood without medication.

After a few months, Taylor began suggesting that I work more on my relationship with food and body image. Since we'd started dating, I had steadily gained about twenty pounds, binge eating alone in the privacy of my apartment when we weren't together. She pointed out how often I weighed myself, critiqued my meals, and called myself "fat." I never felt judged, but her ability to see me clearly was painful, bringing up the necessary dissonance for change. For the most part, I saw our relationship as a crucible for my soul's growth and actualization, but all the philosophizing in the world couldn't propel me beyond the untended wounds of a still-rocky mental terrain. Professional help for disordered eating and body dysmorphia became inevitable.

No amount of discomfort ever swayed my affection for Taylor. In fact, each challenge just further solidified my love for her. Before Taylor, love had been a fantasy, a mirage, some infantile promise of pacification. True love was work, the willingness to be vulnerable, the reward for authentic opening. This love invited Taylor into places I wasn't even aware existed. To be seen, and to stop needing to hide, this was the greatest gift I had ever known. Not even God could love me this way. Taylor's soul was made for mine, and mine for hers. I could taste perfection in the imperfect, and without knowing the path, I saw our destination in absolute love. After six months, I asked her to marry me, and she said yes.

My growing awareness of the relationship between my body image and mood could only have come about through Taylor. The pain of being in my body became excruciating, and I turned anxious, scared that we were making a mistake by getting engaged. I couldn't accept Taylor's love for me, and I grew wary of her motives. She told me she loved my body—she loved me—but I couldn't hear it. I began to find flaws in her in order to justify why she would want to be with me. I imagined she was just ready to get married, that she was settling by being with me. I told myself that she wasn't really in love; she was just in love with the idea of love.

Each time I stepped on the scale, a war was waged in my head. Either Taylor was lying about her attraction to me, or she was lying to herself. I couldn't imagine a scenario where I could gain weight and still be loved. I even called our sex life into question. I doubted whether I was satisfying her, whether I had ever satisfied her, despite her every validation to the contrary.

Once Taylor and I were engaged, our relationship felt like it took on extra pressure. We became strangely afraid of each other, both doubting whether the other would stay, whether the other could stay. The more fixated I became on my weight gain, the more concerned Taylor became about my happiness, and the more she doubted whether or not I was happy, the more fearful she became that I might leave. The relationship grew tense, and we started fighting a lot. This all made me anxious, and so I obsessed more about my body and further doubted Taylor's love.

After a few weeks of shaky communication and bizarre conflict, Taylor came to me one day and sat me down on the couch in my little single-bedroom apartment. We talked about how much we had been fighting. I talked about everything except my body, and the more I talked, the more heartbroken she appeared. She finally took off her engagement ring and said, "If you're going to leave, just go."

Tears started streaming down my face. I couldn't believe what was happening. I was in love. I put the ring back on her finger and told her, "I'm not going anywhere. I love you. I'm going to get help. I'm so sorry."

Our engagement had raised the stakes to the point that I had no other option; it was time to be brave. We decided to go to a few sessions of couples' counseling, and I agreed to see an eating-disorder specialist.

Just to look up Lisa's phone number brought about painful incongruences in my psyche. I was working at AIM House, in my last semester of college, and researching doctoral programs in psychology. I imagined I needed to be fully recovered in order to help others. Reaching out to a therapist felt like the ultimate defeat, but I knew I needed to assassinate my ego if I was ever to have a chance at true love. If I couldn't work things out with Taylor, there was no way I would ever work things out with another person. A life without love was not worth living, and so, with an enormous amount of trepidation, I picked up the phone and made my appointment.

Lisa remembered me from our single session a couple years prior, and she now had a full-time private practice focused solely on eating disorders. My sessions with Lisa were incredibly difficult. Even though I knew she was trained in sensitivity around body-image issues and disordered eating, I still found myself wondering if she was judging me. I also found myself frequently thinking that my problems weren't that big a deal. I would imagine I wasn't very far gone on the eating-disorder spectrum. My ego was constantly playing games, attempting to protect myself from the harsh reality that I was suffering from a full-blown binge-eating disorder and that my views on my body were wrecking my potential marriage.

Lisa suggested that I read a book called *Intuitive Eating*, and I did. It recommended that I trust my intuition around food and hunger, that I stop dieting. It felt extreme, since I had never eaten without adhering to or breaking a strict set of rules, but I agreed to try it. Not dieting was like flipping the off switch to everything I ever knew about eating. My eating had always been all or nothing, either dieting or compulsively overeating and binging. I couldn't fathom eating without restriction. The intuitive-eating model seemed like permission to permanently indulge. I would leave Lisa's office and hit a drive-thru on my way home, rationalizing that my intuition was hungry for a cheeseburger and fries.

Lisa was the first professional whom I talked to in detail about my history of body shame. I told her about the extent to which I felt teased and bullied for being overweight in school. I talked to her about my dieting history, how I constantly attempted to achieve ketosis. I discussed getting liposuction as a teenager. I even talked about my dick. She broke out into laughter the first time I told her about my penis size obsession, telling me that it had never even occurred to her that a man could feel so insecure about this part of his body. Over time, and after reading more information on eating disorders, I realized how traditionally female these issues were. It was nearly impossible for me to find gender-neutral resources, let alone books discussing male-specific treatment.

Regardless of the female focus of the eating-disorder resources, I knew that my concerns were not exclusive to me. Advertisements for penis-enlargement pills were plastered over every porn site I'd ever visited. Diet pills were featured in every supermarket, and many of them targeted men. Dieting books and fitness magazines were consumed by men and women alike. Barbie's body got a lot of media attention, but what about all those shredded superhero action figures I'd grown up playing with? Recovery prompted me to think a lot about the inherent gender issues in eating disorders and body-image obsession. For years now, I'd known that my own ideals of masculinity prevented healing. I began to consider the degree to which men's confusion around masculinity suppressed the detection of eating disorders and body dysmorphia in this half of the population. Additionally, the ideal physique for men differed greatly from that for women, making male eating disorders that much more difficult to detect. In a strange way, coming clean about my eating and body-image struggles felt like the most manly and courageous thing I'd ever done. It took balls.

A few sessions with Lisa provided me with incomprehensible healing. Just being able to talk openly about these ancient wounds allowed me great freedom. At times, it felt emasculating, but emotional work was par for the course at this stage of my recovery. Ignoring my feelings spelled a certain doom, and I was willing to go wherever necessary in order to liberate myself. Taylor and I talked at length about my progress, and she loved me every step of the way. Without her support, I don't know if I would have ever touched these areas. I connected the dots between my childhood, media portrayals of the male physique, my sexual shame, and dieting. I got the point, and so, after only a few months of regular therapy, I declared myself ready to move on.

The difficulty of my work with Lisa was just too great to sustain. Intuitive eating felt impossible. She told me that eating disorder recovery often takes years, and I was quite deflated by the prospect of such an extensive timeline. I started rationalizing that her model didn't work, that intuitive eating was wrong for me. I discovered some recovery ideas that treated binge eating more like addiction, and I pretty much used these models to support the further restriction of sugar and refined carbohydrates, coming full circle to the type of thinking that had landed me in therapy to begin with. I stopped seeing Lisa, and I started trying to abstain from any foods with a high glycemic index. I rationalized that it wasn't disordered anymore, because I wasn't totally restricting carbohydrates.

Just as Lisa and the intuitive eating book had predicted, my abstinence from sugar and its glycemic counterparts invited frequent binging. Even though Taylor had never judged my food choices, I began eating sweets in secret, doing the majority of my eating in the car or while Taylor was at work. I would even go so far as to dispose of any receipts and trash, lest she discover the evidence. Even though my eating hadn't improved much, I did feel more comfortable with my body. I told myself I would be able to heal the rest of the way on my own. I was healthy and productive in most aspects of my life, so I figured I could take it slow with my eating issues.

Most important, Taylor and I were as in love as ever. Having her by my side through this difficult piece of my recovery further affirmed that we were meant to spend the rest of our lives together. If she could love me through this most unlovable part of myself, she could love me through anything. Taylor taught me the meaning of true love, of sacrifice, of commitment. She was the greatest gift God had ever granted me, and I often wondered, *What could I possibly have done to deserve all of this?* Grace is the hardest gift to accept.

Chapter 35

IN SICKNESS AND IN HEALTH

Taylor and I moved in together shortly after I graduated from Naropa University in the spring of 2010. I then began working for a new therapeutic residential program in the small mountain town of Ward, Colorado, twenty miles up from Boulder, called Insight Intensive at Gold Lake. My role was to help with marketing the new program and reaching out to referrals, in addition to working with the young men as the life-skills coach. After a few months, Taylor came on as a lead mentor, and we started working together. Even though I enjoyed my job greatly, I mostly viewed it as a stepping-stone to graduate school; I was determined to eventually become an expert on psychospiritual phenomena.

Since the beginning of my sobriety in 2007, I had developed some pretty alternative views on mental illness, partly founded in my own experience and partly learned in my study of transpersonal psychology. I firmly believed that my past psychotic episodes had been spiritual breakthroughs, cataclysmic shifts in consciousness, and I hoped to help establish the credibility of what some transpersonal psychologists called "spiritual emergencies" in mentally ill patients.

Most pertinent to my convictions around psychosis and mood disturbances was that there were underlying maladaptive cognitive processes and failed belief systems driving madness; that neurological chaos was the symptom, not the cause. This was the primary way I made sense of my history of mania despite being generally stable since removing substance abuse from the equation. I believed my soul had been driving the madness, and now that I was living in spiritual alignment with God and nature, I was more or less healed from symptoms of bipolar disorder.

Over time, I had adopted a number of eclectic spiritual beliefs and practices that might have alarmed my conservative Christian family but didn't call for much concern in the more liberal, alternative town of Boulder, Colorado. I practiced Buddhist meditation, prayed to the God of infinite love, and believed Jesus Christ was humanity's supreme teacher, though not the only one. I practiced some rudimentary qigong and energy-healing exercises, and I even dabbled in various new-age practices, like angel card readings and gemstones. I was also becoming very interested in astrology. Ultimately, I worshiped the unity of the various religious and spiritual practices, believing they all touched on the basic ground of existence as an infinite, creative consciousness.

At the core of humanity was love, and healing depended on the ability to contact this innate wisdom. Much of humanity's suffering was the result of patriarchal aggression, and the movement toward an enlightened society necessitated awakening the feminine principles of unconditional love, abundance, and community. It was far out, and though it might have seemed confusing to an outsider, it felt intuitively right to my soul. Existence was made up of levels of consciousness, movements toward unity. Mental illness, in a spiritual sense, was the perfect soul's attempt to correct confusion, to set straight what had been warped by ignorance and sin; a painful aligning with God toward nondual consciousness.

Taylor and I ended up being engaged for over a year, and we set our wedding date for March 25, 2011. We had endured a fair amount of discomfort, as we set aside our individual neurotic orientations in pursuit of the whole, but we were unwavering in our devotion. Couples' counseling proved paramount in our understanding of how to meet each other's needs while maintaining healthy boundaries. We could see that our commitment required much more growth than our single lives or dating demanded of us. Love was the invitation to go deeper, the challenge to stay present, and the faith that we could be there for each other where others in the past could not.

My recovery seemed complicated, but over the years, I had just come to think of myself as an eccentric, spiritual, sensitive man. I was entering my fourth year of sobriety, and there were still no obvious indications that I needed treatment for bipolar disorder. I was aware that regulating my mood had become a complex endeavor. My stability required everything from minimizing my coffee intake, to maintaining my meditation routine, to scheduling sleep, to ingesting just the right amount of nicotine, to guarding myself against Taylor's every minor deviation in tone or body language. My recently discovered eating disorder troubles only complicated the mess, and I could see that I got more or less moody depending on what I ate and how I felt about it.

My parents couldn't have been prouder of how far I had come, and they were totally in love with Taylor. Still, they remained on guard about my apparently dormant bipolar condition. When I brought Taylor home for a visit, Mom privately pulled her aside to ask, "Taylor, has Chris talked to you about his bipolar disorder?"

Taylor knew everything, but just as I did, she believed my episodes were due to alcoholism and addiction. I assured Taylor, "I really don't think we have anything to worry about. It just makes Mom and Dad feel better to think all my problems are from chemical imbalances. That way, they don't have to question their parenting."

When it came time for Taylor and me to tie the knot, we were ready, not because everything was perfect, but because we were willing to spend the rest of our lives being imperfect together. The best part about our wedding was planning the ceremony. Being free spirits, and wanting to put my transpersonal psychology wisdom to work, we decided to create a custom wedding ceremony. The theme was the circle, a symbol denoting completion, eternity, and unity.

We took two weeks off, spending a week in Maui for our wedding, then traveling to Fiji for a weeklong honeymoon. The festivities went off without a hitch, and our wedding was nothing short of mystical. Even the Mormons and the Catholics loved it! I could feel God blessing our lives, and to have all of our loved ones gathered together in support of us was inspiring, spiritually and emotionally. The ceremony felt more sacred than we could have ever intended, as our family and friends circled around us, offered their blessings, and witnessed our vows to love each other forever. The impact of our ceremony resonated more deeply with my soul than anything I had ever experienced.

In the couple of days leading up to our nuptials, I developed a minor respiratory infection. It wasn't a big deal, but I took some antibiotics and used my inhaler regularly in the hopes that it would pass. I finished my antibiotics course with no problems at all, and my breathing and congestion improved, though a little discomfort remained heading into our honeymoon. Over the next few days, while we were supposed to be having exotic, romantic adventures on private Fijian beaches, I grew increasingly fatigued. I tried to determine the source of my sudden melancholy. Was it emotional exhaustion from our wedding week? Something I ate? Was I sick? I didn't feel like myself.

When we got back to Boulder, my respiratory infection returned, but I needed to get back to work after the two weeks I'd already taken for the wedding and honeymoon. I tried to tough it out and was prescribed some corticosteroids, which would hopefully expedite my return to health. Immediately, my breathing improved, but getting back to work felt really hectic. To be expected with a new program, there had been a few organizational changes and new hires in the two weeks we'd been gone. I was needed more in the milieu, only a slight departure from my desk duties.

Over the first couple of days back, the hectic feeling of returning transformed into total chaos. I grew agitated about the recent minor changes, and I started getting extremely frustrated. I became obsessed with the idea that my program director should be fired, and I mouthed off to my boss about his recent and obvious errors. I suddenly felt like the company's success was entirely up to me. I e-mailed coworkers, some individually and some in select groups, degrading what I believed were failed organizational structures, challenging people's leadership capabilities, and questioning the integrity of the entire company. I was called into a couple of meetings and given the benefit of the doubt, where my complaints were slightly validated, and my superiors generally encouraged me to get on board and be a team player, but I couldn't shake my extraordinary agitation. Taylor would ask me what was going on, and I'd spout off a long list of built-up grievances and petty resentments since my hire nearly a year before.

I had difficulty sleeping, but I assumed my last few restless nights were the result of jet lag. I was the most tired and wired I could ever remember being. By the end of the week, I was absolutely irate. No one could do their job right, and I was feeling like I should be promoted to run the company, lest the entire operation burn to the ground. I was disruptive and outspoken, constantly complaining to any coworker who would listen. I started threatening to quit if I didn't get my way. The most bizarre part was that I was making up all of it; the only legit grievance, if any, was that my schedule had changed.

Taylor approached me for a serious talk, in which she expressed concern over how worked up I was getting, and while she was describing my sudden extreme behavior, I realized what was happening: *I'm going manic.* I had heard about how steroids could induce psychosis, and this frightening epiphany shook me to the core. I immediately stopped taking the medication, but it was too late.

Taylor knew about my history of psychosis and what was eventually considered an inconclusive bipolar diagnosis, but nothing could have prepared her for what I knew might be coming. I sat her down, wide-eyed with heightened intensity: "You need to listen to me carefully. I don't know how much longer I'm going to be coherent. I'm losing touch with reality. Whatever you do, don't tell my parents. They'll just make everything worse."

She looked terrified. I grabbed her hands. "Look at me, baby. You have to trust me. I'm going to try and sleep it off."

Then shortly after telling Taylor to keep my secret, I ended up calling my parents myself, and confessing that I wasn't feeling right. Although I tried to downplay the severity, Mom jumped on a flight from Atlanta only a few hours after getting off the phone with me.

Dad called. "Chris, Mom is just going to come in case things escalate. Just think of it as a visit. I'm sure everything will be fine."

I was already getting paranoid, adamant that I didn't want her to come: "Dad, you don't get it, she is going to be the reason things escalate! She's going to scare Taylor! She's going to stress me out!"

I hung up on my dad and started drafting contracts for Taylor to sign, in the event that I lost control of my treatment. I insisted, "Sign this contract with me, so you get to make decisions in the event that they deem me unable to make decisions for myself."

I thought I was making perfect sense, but Taylor looked at me like I was speaking a foreign language.

She started to cry. "I'm scared."

I hugged her. "I'm scared too. Listen, we are going to be fine. I just need to sleep. Mom has always wanted me to be bipolar; I'm just having a medical reaction to steroids. I don't want to get hospitalized."

The main reason I didn't want my mom to show up was that I didn't want to take any medicine. I equated psychotropic medication with months of lethargy, depression, and rapid weight gain. Not only that, but psychotropic medication was for bipolar patients, and after years of pharmaceutical-free living, I knew God had healed me of my afflictions, and nothing was going to change that.

The stage was set. *This is bigger than my mood, bigger than my sanity, bigger than my life, bigger than my marriage. This is about God. This is about my soul. This is about letting karma work itself out, about trusting the Holy Spirit and staying receptive to reality, no matter the circumstances. Medication means that God is wrong, and I know the truth. Psychotropics are the perverse creations of men, men who don't have faith in God's workings, men who believe the divine to be nothing but the delusional creation of neurological misfiring.* I was gone.

My education and training weren't doing me any favors, as all of my knowledge and comprehension of spirituality and psychology merged into the ultimate weapon for denial. I started drafting pages and pages of my own treatment plan, explaining that I was in the midst of a spiritual emergency, that I was not psychotic, and outlining the necessary components of my successful navigation back to homeostasis without medication. I even listed instructions for hospital staff, in the event that I ended up in the psych ward.

When I went outside for a cigarette break, I saw a hawk flying low, and I watched as it flew high into the sky. Right as the hawk got so far that I could see only a speck of black, a plane flew underneath. In that moment, I suddenly knew without any doubt that God had put me on this path to take on the mental-health system, right the wrongs of mental-illness treatment, and use my healing as a case that would eventually establish proper treatment of psychosis as a spiritual emergency. This was the divine intervention of soul wisdom, of God-union, of kundalini, of satori. This would be my opportunity to prove my enlightenment, and in turn, enlighten a world in need of spiritual attunement. The hawk was the symbol, the revealing of the Christ and the beginning of the end. *I will return humanity to natural order and usher in a new heaven and a new earth. No manmade chemicals can cure God's perfect creation.*

So, in only a week since my honeymoon, over five years since my last hospitalization, I was once again experiencing an acute manic episode, albeit facilitated by a course in corticosteroids. I suddenly hated a job I loved. I believed my mom, who had always supported me and was dropping everything to fly out and help me, was going to try to lock me up in the insane asylum and throw away the key. Worst of all, I was trying to convince Taylor that she couldn't trust anyone, least of all my parents and medical doctors.

Once the mania took hold, I lost the power of reason, except to reinforce this overwhelming delusional grandeur, the idea that I was the chosen one. I was, once again, going out of my mind, feeling as though I'd never known reality prior to now. My entire system was shocked, and I was now convinced that God Himself had led me to this point, so that once and for all, I could fulfill my divine purpose, my soul's calling, the reason I was put on earth. All those times in the hospital were just God's way of preparing me for this moment. It didn't matter that I was educated or trained on these issues, or that I had once upon a time been open to an accurate bipolar diagnosis. My whole life, my entire worldview, now depended on me *not* being bipolar, and I was ready to fight to the death.

Chapter 36

LOCKDOWN

The more time went on, the clearer my mission became. I was ready to attain full enlightenment, permanent samadhi. I knew I was sick, but I believed it was solely the result of side effects from the corticosteroids, and since there were no coincidences and everything happened for a reason, I believed this was nevertheless God's path for me. I was ready and willing to pursue the hidden, divine significance of my circumstances.

This time, I wouldn't let anyone interrupt my spiritual unfoldment with powerful psychotropics. I understood that my past psychotic episodes were botched attempts at ultimate awakening, that psychiatric treatment interrupted my total God-realization. In order for enlightenment to take place, I would need everyone's full cooperation and support. I began to disclose my revelations to Taylor and Mom, providing as much information as I felt their limited minds could comprehend.

The most important part of allowing this process to unfold would be staying out of the hospital. If I got locked up, they'd try to drug me and I'd miss my opportunity for nirvana. My family was obviously concerned. Even in my delusional state, I understood how frightened everyone was. They pleaded with me to get help, and the next day, I agreed to see a psychiatrist, albeit just to prove to them that I was indeed sane. "You still don't get it," I insisted. "One has to lose his mind to truly find himself."

I knew they'd try to lock me up. To cover all my bases, I packed a suitcase. In it, I placed about a dozen spiritual and psychological books to study, my sketchbook and crayons for colorful note taking, and multiple copies of my treatment instructions for any staff planning on trying to midwife the birth of my highest self. I gave Taylor a list of my former professors, friends, and colleagues who I knew were somewhat familiar with spiritual emergency, so that they could assist her in understanding and help me regain stability once the Spirit had run its course.

Taylor had to go to work, so her sister and brother-in-law came over to help my mom get me to the hospital. I picked out my garments for our trip to Boulder Community Hospital's emergency department, choosing my blue shirt with an image of a Smurf astronaut, with the words SPACED OUT in bold across the top. It seemed the appropriate choice. Completing the uniform were gym shorts, Uggs, and my large black designer peacoat. I felt constantly overstimulated by conversation, and so I used a big red pair of headphones to cancel out the minutiae. I was prepared to enlighten everyone on how to help my soul and nervous system realign. A warrior heeding the call, I was ready for battle.

When we all arrived at the hospital, my paranoia amped up, and I immediately regretted agreeing to go. I interrogated the intake person, explaining that I had a right to know when I was being admitted and at exactly which point I would be forfeiting my rights to leave of my own accord. They had the power to hold me against my will, and I asked every person I talked to about my rights. I collected multiple copies of their patient-rights brochures and studied them while I waited. With a great deal of assurance from the staff and my family, I was eventually escorted to my hospital room. With no word yet as to when they would be able to take away my freedom, I remained on edge, growing in my belligerence and intensity, jotting notes down about the staff's behaviors and answers to my concerns, in the event I needed to pursue legal recourse.

I was told I wouldn't be seeing a psychiatrist, and the second I started getting evaluated by the nurse, I became increasingly convinced that I would need to sue the hospital for malpractice and violation of my rights. On my little brochures, I circled all of the rights that were being violated, and the nurse grew annoyed by the amount of defensiveness and cross-examination. I knew the evaluation was like a test of my sanity, and I needed to pass in order to get out of there alive. In my mind, the more legal jargon I threw around, and the more I pretended to know my rights, the less likely they were to order my hospitalization, but surely, I was just making matters worse.

We were there so long that Taylor was able to finish her shift and meet up with all of us. Her sister's husband got me food while we waited for word of what would happen next. I eventually finished the nurse's psychiatric evaluation, and we all anxiously awaited the results.

After a few more hours, the nurse came into my room and informed me that I would be allowed to go home, but she insisted that I needed to see a psychiatrist first thing in the morning. I agreed. Shocked and relieved, I immediately began to weep, thanking my family for supporting me and promising them I would get help. It was as if the safety of knowing I wouldn't be hospitalized allowed for some clarity to emerge. I was going to be okay. For their part, my family was enormously relieved to hear me agree to see a psychiatrist and acknowledge that I needed help. All they really wanted was for me to see a doctor.

A few minutes into my tear-filled conversation with my family in the hospital room, the nurse came back in and told me that she had just talked to the on-call psychiatrist, and I was now being placed on a seventy-two-hour hold. She apologized for the confusion. We were stunned.

"You can't do that!" I cried. "No one ever told me this was a possibility; I have rights!"

Even my family argued on my behalf: "But he just agreed to see someone in the morning."

None of our pleading mattered. I was told the police would be involved if I tried to leave the hospital. They moved me into another room and told me to say good-bye to my family. Taylor and I embraced, assuring each other that everything was going to be okay, but we were both terrified.

Whatever sanity had come through disappeared immediately upon the news that I was being placed on a seventy-two-hour hold. I threatened to sue, accusing the staff of malpractice. I started e-mailing myself on my iPhone, writing down everything that happened, thinking that if I documented it, I could use the information later in court. I imagined I was in a civil rights battle, that they were stripping me of my freedom.

"You never told me I could be held against my will!" I shouted.

I even read, in one of their pamphlets, that they had to tell me when I was entering their care. I was positive that they were breaking the law. I put all of the hospital documents and declarations of my rights in a folder and included it in my suitcase with all of my books and clothes.

This is my life's purpose, I thought. *How many patients have had this happen to them and can't do anything about it? How many people are victims of this sort of abuse? They shouldn't be able to get away with this. I don't need medication. I don't need to get locked up. I need to get in touch with my heart and soul. I need comfort. I need safety.* A psych ward was the last place I wanted to go.

There were no open beds in Boulder, so after being at the hospital for what seemed like forever, I was strapped down to a gurney and escorted in an ambulance to West Pines, another hospital outside of Denver. I still felt coherent enough, but I knew I needed to sleep. The hospital staff explained to me that I would see a psychiatrist first thing in the morning and would then have the opportunity to get discharged.

Okay, I thought, *I can do this.*

One night in the psych ward, and then I'd be out in the morning. They would see that I was sane, that I'd had an adverse reaction to steroids, and they'd allow me to go home. I could sue the hospital for wrongly placing me on a seventy-two-hour hold later.

By the time I arrived at West Pines, I was angry that it was already the middle of the night. I complained to the staff, "How am I supposed to heal myself if y'all won't even let me sleep?"

Once inside the hospital, I was instantly reminded why I didn't want to be put on hold. There were crazy people everywhere. I started asking the staff how they were going to keep me safe, and they just kept assuring me that I would be okay.

They showed me to a dark room where a stranger was occupying the far bed, and despite my resistance and fear of being harmed, I finally fell asleep. In the morning, I was woken up by hospital staff telling me that it was time for me to see the psychiatrist.

How dare they wake me up after keeping me awake all night? I thought to myself. *Don't they know I need my sleep?* I was furious. The thought that I was being mistreated, that I was the victim of numerous crimes against humanity, intensified. I was ready to give them an earful about these clear injustices.

I sat down with a psychiatrist and psychologist, anxious to set them straight about the whole mishap. Before we could even get past introductions, I started telling them what happened. I told them that I was a mental-health professional, that this was all a big mistake, that I'd had an adverse reaction to steroid medication. "I don't need to be here. I don't need medication. I just need to sleep, something your staff is repeatedly preventing me from doing this morning."

After about one minute of my ranting, the psychiatrist bluntly asserted, "You're manic and you need medication."

I was pissed. "You just met me. You can't tell me I'm manic. You woke me up from sleep. A manic person wouldn't have been sleeping. You can't diagnose me. You don't know anything about me!"

He rebuffed me, saying, "I've been doing this for years. It only takes me about a minute to diagnose mania."

I took a deep breath, desperate to keep it together, and pleaded with them: "Listen, I just got married. I'm missing work. I need to get out of here. I'm not bipolar. I'm suffering from a steroid side effect."

The psychologist replied, "I'm sorry, but we're not lifting your hold."

I was furious: "This is bullshit! I'm not taking your medication. You can't keep me here forever. I know my rights. This is illegal. I have the right to an attorney!"

The whole ordeal felt so cold and impersonal—in the moment, and in retrospect too. I was heartbroken. I had just married the love of my life, and I was scared of losing her. I was scared of losing my job. I was scared my career was over. All I had done was take medication for a respiratory infection, and now I was going insane. I deserved to be heard.

The second the psychiatrist mocked me, I was gone, willing to fight to the end for my right to a humane approach, one that recognized there was a soul in here. What angered me the most was that the doctors acted as if I were stupid, as if I were just wasting their time. They were so dismissive. They didn't even try to talk me through my treatment plan or give me any idea of how they could help. They didn't seem to care at all. They could hardly even be troubled to look up from their clipboards. I had been waiting since yesterday to see a doctor, and they barely sat down before walking away from the table.

I was going to show them. This was war.

Chapter 37

KINGDOM COME

I had the right to refuse medication, for now. My case manager explained to me the lengthy process of getting discharged if I was not going to comply with treatment. My psychiatrist could order an extension on my hold by declaring me gravely disabled, and it would be days until I could get assigned a court date to defend my sanity. Only then would I have the opportunity to leave if a judge ruled in my favor.

Multiple staff members assured me, "Patients never win." Their attempts to discourage me felt threatening. They went out of their way to explain what would happen if the judge didn't side with me. I would be forced to take medication, and if I wouldn't take it orally, they would forcibly inject it into me.

The staff painted a grim image of my demise, but it only served to fuel my fight. I could see the future. They'd write about my case in the history books, a landmark ruling, no doubt resulting in the legal establishment of greater rights and more humane treatment for mentally ill patients. I would be a hero. My childhood fantasies of being a civil rights leader were being fulfilled.

"You are pathologizing mystical revelation and diagnosing God as a delusion!" I declared. "I'm not a danger to anyone or myself. This is religious persecution!"

Mania had me caught somewhere between fantasy and reality, in something of a fantastical reality. Every thought and emotion seemed so much more intense than it needed to be, and every interaction served only to validate my delusions. My rights might have been violated, but my defiant attitude was creating unnecessary tension.

As each day passed, staff asked me if I was still noncompliant, and when I confirmed my stance, they would assure me that my court hearing would not work out in my favor. We were at a standoff, in which they kept threatening to keep me longer and I kept threatening to sue. Most of the staff started ignoring me; others grew agitated.

I started writing down everything in preparation for my court case and eventual lawsuit. I documented all of the staff's inadequacies, how they disrespected patients, how they were mistreating me. I became incredibly vocal and confrontational about my perceived injustice, constantly calling staff out for their "induction" throughout the milieu, using clinical terms in an attempt to point out their incompetence and inflate my expertise. I reported behavior to their supervisors and coworkers. I would approach the psychiatrists with my notepad in hand and ask, "Is it appropriate for your staff to yell in the faces of psychotic patients?"

I started rallying my fellow patients around our lack of basic rights, claiming the hospital was providing inhumane living conditions.

"Even prison inmates get to go outside for fresh air," I announced. "What kind of barbaric system keeps people locked indoors for days at a time? What are we, caged rats?"

Patients weren't allowed to drink coffee, listen to music, or smoke cigarettes. All of my vices were stripped away. Smoking had recently been banned in the hospital, so nicotine patches were prescribed, but they didn't seem to help. Outdoor activity and cafeteria visits were privileges, earned only through compliance with treatment, something I was refusing. I was stuck in this one large room with two hallways leading to bedrooms. The only people to talk to were employees, who were ignoring me, and psychotic patients, who hardly made any sense. It felt like torture.

I found a way to get in touch with the clinical director of the hospital by calling his office from the patient phone. I left him a message, telling him my situation and reporting a number of his staff members for what I considered to be patient abuse. When he came to meet me on the floor of the psych ward, I pleaded with him to help me get released. I told him that I knew I was having problems, but I didn't need to be there, and I didn't need medication. I threatened him: "Listen. Your staff is undertrained. Get me out of here, or I'm going to dysregulate this entire milieu."

He was a very kind man, and he did his best to talk me down. Up until that point, no one else had listened to me for more than five minutes. I said, "I know how this looks, but I'm not far gone enough to be here. I want to go home to my wife. You and I both know psychotic patients can't reason like this or see another person's point of view. This is a mistake. I shouldn't be here." It was Friday, and he agreed to come see me again after the weekend. He encouraged me to hang in there, and to please not act out in the ways I was threatening.

I tried to stay calm, but a couple more days in the psych ward was all I needed to jump off the edge of sanity into the infinite abyss of manic psychosis. By the time the director returned on Monday, I was dead set on my mission. I looked to some of my heroes: Martin Luther King Jr., Gandhi, Jesus. They were all civil rights activists, all radicals for their causes. This was my battle. I was going to fight the system if it killed me. They had no right to withhold fresh air, sunshine, and exercise. They had no right to force me to take medication when I wasn't suicidal or threatening harm to others. I started gearing up for court. I recorded all the laws I thought they might be breaking, all the rights they were stripping from the patients under their care.

I converted my two-patient room into a solo retreat sanctuary. My roommate was discharged, and every time the janitor made the bed, I would throw all the sheets into the hallway to ensure I could have the room to myself. I set up the beds to allow for enough space for walking meditation, and I would pace about the room, trying to ground myself, and praying for God to reveal what He was asking of me. I draped a sheet over the bedside table, where I stacked my books and some drawings and placed a few miscellaneous food items in circular arrangements to create my altar. I would alternate between sitting meditation, walking meditation, prayer, and song, trying to allow for the kundalini to work itself out.

After a few more days of defiance, I started relishing my role as a civil rights savior. I was a force to be reckoned with, no doubt. I started antagonizing the hospital staff, my way of using nonviolent protest. I made constant requests, most of which went unmet. I made as many demands as I could that I believed to be within my rights, relishing any time that they went unnoticed, thinking that I could use this information against them in court. I demanded spiritual counsel. I demanded to speak with a psychotherapist. I demanded to breathe fresh air and feel the sun on my skin. They kept insisting that I needed to comply and attend the groups in order to get signed off for those privileges. I educated them: "You don't get it. These aren't patient privileges. These are human rights!"

I started attending the groups but mostly just to point out the inadequacies of the staff. I complained about how rude and confrontational they were with other patients. I questioned everything they did.

Some of the staff pulled me aside and tried to reason with me. They told me, "These patients need help, and you're interfering with their treatment." They threatened to put me in solitary confinement.

"Go ahead, put me in solitary, please. It'll be the perfect place to meditate. Is it quiet in there? Can I go right now?"

I started ramping up my efforts, incessantly pressing the HELP button in my room as an act of protest. I would sit in my meditation posture on the bed and wait for staff to come rushing in. One of them grew so angry that he pushed me up against the wall. As scared as I was, I felt like I was winning. The staff was clearly on tilt, the patients were joining me in my complaints, and it was only a matter of time before I could prove my sanity and pursue legal action against the hospital.

When Taylor would visit during the evenings, I'd insist that she drain our bank accounts and hire a lawyer.

"Notify the news outlets. Post what's happening on Facebook and Twitter. Tell all my friends to come see me. This is a crime against humanity. I'm not dangerous. My seventy-two hours are up. This shit is illegal!"

Taylor always said the same thing: "Just take their medicine, so you can get out of here, and then we can talk about all that."

I refused. "I can't. I won't. They're trying to give me Xanax; I'm sober!"

She was so sad. "Chris, how long do you plan on doing this?" she asked.

I felt bad, but not bad enough: "As long as it takes, babe. This is criminal. Do you know how many people this probably happens to? Not everyone has the education and training I do to take on the system. This is my duty. I have a civic responsibility!"

I was growing increasingly psychotic, something I rationalized was just the result of my soul aligning with God. I spent a great deal of time alone in my room. It was my safe space. I rearranged my furniture to create a sort of fortress, so staff couldn't enter without knocking. I configured the food on my altar to provide healing. I placed almonds in the shape of a cross, put my orange in the center, and stacked little packages of cheese, eating the food after a few hours as if I were absorbing extra spiritual energy it had gathered on the altar. I counted out tiles on the floor and began walking in a particular pattern around my room, convinced my walking meditation was connecting me to the universe. In my mind, I was growing more and more powerful with the spiritual energy of God-realization. I believed I was becoming superhuman.

I could feel a profound wisdom permeating my being. I was inspired to don my spiritual dress, looking into the bathroom mirror and telling myself, "If they want crazy, I'll show them crazy." I took shaving cream and slicked back my hair. I used one of the hospital's blue Crayola markers to draw tribal symbols on my face. I wrapped the bed's white blankets around my neck and draped towels around my waist like a loincloth. I was connecting to my ancestral roots, some ancient shamanic energy of eons past. I continued marking up my body, drawing symbols all over my arms. I could see my incarnations. I was a shaman, king of the ancient enlightened city of Shambhala, Buddha, Christ, the last avatar to set humanity on its righteous course. I wasn't sure what to call the Source, but I knew it was ancient, as old as time itself.

I informed my case manager that I refused to work with men any longer, telling her that they triggered me and made me feel unsafe. I made up that I'd been raped and that the male staff was reminding me of buried childhood trauma. What I really believed was that the men were more unconscious, less in touch with the divine feminine energy working its way through my body. The men were more commonly threatening me, invading my space, and raising their voices. My request was granted, and I started working with a female psychiatrist. I liked her energy much better than that of the Neanderthal who had diagnosed me in sixty seconds.

An entire week had passed, and it was still unclear how I was going to get out. The longer I stayed at West Pines, the more comfortable I became, and the more calculated I was in my fight against the system. I made a sign for my door that read KNOCK AND THE DOOR SHALL BE OPENED, and I ignored requests to keep my entry clear of furniture. Anytime they asked anything of me, I would ask to see my lawyer. I would interrupt conversations between staff members and the patients. When one of the doctors explained to a patient that his bipolar diagnosis was like having diabetes and his medication was like taking insulin, I objected: "You can measure blood-sugar levels. You can't measure brain chemistry. That analogy is bullshit. Don't lie to him, doctor."

I paused my unruly behavior only for family visits. When I knew that Taylor was coming, I would take a shower, change my clothes, wash the markings off my face, and do my best to feign normalcy. There was still a conscious part of my mind that was scared to lose her, afraid to let her see what was happening to me, a part desperate to assure her that everything would be okay.

My family pleaded with me to take the medication so I could just get out of there. They could see that I was getting worse, and they were just as convinced as I was that the hospital setting was doing more harm than good. Taylor was the only leverage that worked on me. My dad had flown out to be with my mom and Taylor, and my parents visited me one day alone while Taylor was at work. They told me, "Taylor is really upset. She needs you to come out."

I had spent over a week in the hospital without medication when the court date was finally set. It was further impressed upon me, by my family, that I needed to at least take something if I was going to have any chance of leaving the hospital. The only reason I even considered it was because I felt bad for Taylor. I talked with my psychiatrist about considering meds, ordering her to give me printouts of the medicines' various side effects, so I could come to an educated decision. I ended up bargaining to take the mildest one, called Tegretol, if she would just grant me the privilege to go outside when the staff took patients on walks. She consented, and so did I.

As the Tegretol began to kick in, I started using my imprisonment to delve into psychospiritual theory. Revelations poured into my psyche like a raging river. I tried to keep up, frantically scribbling down notes and drawing endless pictures and graphs. My ultimate realization was outlined in a chart of enlightenment, integrating spiritual and emotional phenomena. I stayed up all night etching my final masterpiece with crayons on the floor tiles in my room.

I could see the basis of all wisdom traditions. *The soul begets a body and mind, which comes into union with nature, realizing God beyond itself, and ultimately achieving nondual consciousness, the nirvana of enlightenment, where God and the individual become one. The soul causes sadness, the body causes fear, the mind causes anger, relationships cause love, God-realization causes joy, and nondual consciousness causes nirvana. The individual self is the source of all suffering!* This was the key to merging psychological and spiritual theory. I had solved the puzzle. *At last, eureka!*

Chapter 38

JUDGMENT DAY

The Tegretol seemed to take just enough of the edge off for me to get serious about leaving, and once I was allowed greater hospital privileges, I began to feel more like myself again. I think my treatment team started getting scared about all of my legal threats, because the second I started popping those pills and stopped my little nonviolent protests, they gave me whatever I asked for, even though none of my views changed. I was switched out of the acute wing of the hospital and allowed to take cafeteria trips, leave for day visits with my family, go for walks, and see spiritual counselors—all the requests I had been making since my arrival. I was playing the game, determined to get released, return to my life, and eventually file a lawsuit against Boulder Community Hospital and West Pines for my wrongful hospitalization.

First things first: I needed a judge to order my release from West Pines. I had spent all my time preparing to sue—making daily logs, recording conversations, and photocopying random documents—but back in reality, I was the defendant, not them. My court date was approaching, so I tried to stay on my best behavior.

I had a couple of phone calls with my public defender, and we needed to find an expert who would testify on my behalf. Although I was able to get Lisa to consider, we ended up deciding that my father, a medical doctor, would be the best option. The hope was that if Dad could explain corticosteroid-induced psychosis to the judge, then the court might rule in my favor.

My family delivered all the necessary garb for me to look professional. I needed to look sharp if I was to have any chance of beating the system. I had only one shot at avoiding indefinite detention and forced medication.

After twelve days of hospitalization, judgment day had finally arrived. I showered, shaved, and got all dressed up in my suit and tie. I felt like I was in a Hollywood makeover scene. A bunch of my fellow patients mocked my efforts, telling me their stories of losing out, but one of the nurses encouraged me, saying, "This was wrong, Chris. Your case is the kind that deserves to win. I'm pulling for you." I just knew I was going to make history, that my ruling would set a precedent to change laws all across the nation.

A police officer came to escort me. He cuffed my hands and feet and attached the cuffs to chains. They had me ride in the back of an armored police truck, all the way to the Boulder County Court.

"I'm not wearing a seat belt, officer," I mocked. "I guess mental-health patients don't have a right to safe travel either?"

Even on my way to judgment, I was still antagonistic. All authority needed to be held accountable.

"I am not a criminal, sir. I am not a danger. You'll see. Remember my name, Chris Cole. I'll be the one spearheading the equal rights movement for mentally ill patients. The end of this injustice is near."

When we arrived at the courthouse, I felt like a prisoner on death row. My lawyer warned me to say as little as possible, that it would be up to the judge whether or not I would testify. She and I squabbled over the benefits of my possible call to the stand. I thought my testimony would be nothing short of the miraculous word of God, and she disagreed: "Listen, this judge is tough. Don't speak unless spoken to, and only answer the questions asked."

"When will West Pines answer for their malpractice?" I asked.

She lowered her glasses and looked me in the eye. "This case is just to defend you."

To my disappointment, the courtroom looked much less glamorous than I had imagined. There was no jury, no reporters, and no audience at all except for my family. As we had discussed, Dad was called as an expert witness. He talked about how psychosis is a well-documented side effect of corticosteroids, that I was a victim of medication, and that I could and should be released to my family in order to continue care outside of the hospital. He assured the judge that I was not in any danger, and that my family was more than capable of caring for me in an outpatient setting.

Despite the testimony of my psychiatrist, that I was still manic and that I should stay under care of the hospital and be forced to take medication, the judge ruled in my favor, and I was released on the spot without ever having to testify. The officer removed my chains. My lawyer was excited, as if she'd just won a neighborhood tennis match. She explained to me how rare it was for a case like mine to be won.

I immediately asked her, "How do I go about the next steps?" She didn't understand, so I explained my plan to sue for damages.

She softly touched my shoulder. "You and your family have been through a lot. Just be grateful to be out of there, and go take care of yourself."

I was insulted by her suggestion. "Just give me your card, please. This system took everything from me. Someone deserves to be held accountable."

I was so fired up when I left the courthouse that day. It was all surreal. After nearly two weeks of trying to get out of the hospital, I was finally freed. I couldn't believe it happened. Taylor was crying. We were all crying. I couldn't even imagine the level of disturbance my new wife must have been feeling. I desperately tried to make sense of what had occurred, and I became increasingly convinced that this was God's plan for me, that I had been placed in this position in order to change laws and bring about more humane treatment of helpless, mentally ill patients.

I rode with Taylor back to West Pines, to pick up my belongings and complete my discharge. I wanted to paint my face just to antagonize the staff, but Taylor wouldn't let me. I still didn't understand how much pain I had put her through.

Upon my entry to the hospital, I made sure to let all the staff know I had won. I was gloating, high from my little victory, slightly vindicated, proud to be deemed sane enough to rejoin civilization.

When Taylor and I got home, I started going through all of my documentation from my stay at the hospital. I outlined how they'd broken laws and patient rights, creating a huge binder full of notes. I started calling lawyers to get representation. I continued to beg Taylor to take out all of her savings in order to pay for legal fees, attempting to convince her that we would make the money back tenfold.

I pleaded with her: "This is going to be like *Brown v. Board of Education*, babe. This isn't about me. This is about the millions of mentally ill patients who don't have a voice, who don't have resources. They need better care, better treatment than this."

My employers at Insight Intensive encouraged me to take as much time as I needed. Though I might not have been psychotic any longer, I was still borderline delusional, just as obsessed with legal recourse and imagining my eventual vindication, fame, and monetary compensation. When Taylor would leave for work, I would stay home and research how to file a lawsuit.

Every lawyer I talked to advised me against legal action. They talked about how expensive it was. They talked about how long the process would be. They told me they only represented people who had been rendered severely handicapped during their confinement or the family of deceased relatives. There was no hope for representation, but I desperately needed the hospital to answer for their wrongs. I needed to be right, to know that all this pain meant something. I needed to justify my sanity, to have my plight validated. *I've been mistreated. I've been victimized.* I couldn't let it go.

Once all the attorneys rejected my case, I began tirelessly notifying the media about my story, determined to expose the grave injustices and discrimination against personal spiritual practices and beliefs. I figured if I could get some publicity, then lawyers or advocacy groups might pick up my case pro bono.

The media never responded to my e-mails. I was totally defeated, unable to tell which way was up. For me, it was either all or nothing. I was spiritual or crazy, brilliant or mad, in the right or in the wrong. I was so confused, still coming back into reality, certain my life could never be the same. I truly believed I had been wronged, but as time went on, and with the help of Taylor, I also saw that I had been totally out of my mind. I was ready to plead temporary insanity, but it was only because I took those damn corticosteroids. *Otherwise,* I thought, *none of this would have ever happened.*

Chapter 39

RESURRECTION

I stopped taking the Tegretol, believing I no longer needed medication. I thought my steroid-induced psychosis had run its course and left me with what was sure to be immeasurable wisdom and purpose. God worked in mysterious ways, so I rationalized the whole episode the best I could, trusting that accidental enlightenment was still enlightenment nonetheless.

I had already heard it a thousand times: "What goes up must come down."

Sanity inevitably returned, but it came at the steep price of deep depression. My fruitless search for legal representation and media exposure left me bitter and resentful. Not only was I mad at the hospital, but I was angry at my family, believing it was their fault that I'd gotten so manic: if they hadn't come to Colorado, I wouldn't have been pushed to see a doctor, and I might have come down naturally on my own. I was even resentful of Taylor, thinking if it weren't for her, I would still be in the hospital, protesting, fighting for the rights of the people, carrying out God's vision for me.

There was so much fear underneath my resentments. I was afraid that all this suffering was for naught, that my supposed revelations were just delusions, narcissistic plays of my childhood repressions. I feared that I might just be the victim of Ken Wilber's "pre/trans fallacy"—that my supposed ego transcendence was really just a lack of ego formation. I feared I wasn't enlightened, that I was just an egomaniac. I feared that I shouldn't work in the psychotherapeutic field, that my hopes of pursuing graduate training were irresponsible. But my biggest fear, the one I was most afraid to touch, was that Taylor regretted marrying me.

The more rational I became, the more I could see the futility of my whole civil rights shtick. I might have been wronged, but I had definitely been psychotic, and the amount of effort it would require to pursue legal action was nearly incomprehensible, not to mention my declarations of spiritual emergency seemed all too self-gratifying. Eventually, I gave up. If nothing else, I grew tired of the rejection. Closing the books on my legal recourse felt defeating, and I realized my time in the hospital had been a waste. A silent rage consumed me as my mind became engulfed in layers of bewilderment. God was nowhere to be found, and my body was failing me. The gates of heaven slammed shut, leaving me stranded.

My depression gained momentum, and with every heavy breath, I sank deeper into lethargy and despair. I was losing all hope. I tried going back to my job at Insight Intensive, but returning to work proved to be impossible. Between the e-mails, calls, and fiery rants, every coworker knew I had "lost my mind." It was humiliating. I was supposed to be the one helping people, not the one needing help. I lasted only a couple of weeks before breaking down to my boss, crying, and telling him I didn't want to work there anymore. I started trying to get therapy for what I considered to be post-traumatic stress from the hospitalization. I can't even begin to describe how painful it was to suddenly have gone psychotic after all these years, especially right after getting married.

I found myself feeling as lost as I'd ever been. For years, I'd operated under the belief that God had cured me of bipolar disorder and addiction. I felt as if God had betrayed me. How could I ask Taylor to stay married to a psychopath? How could I pursue my dream of studying psychospiritual phenomena if I wasn't healed myself? I couldn't even imagine a life on mood-stabilizing drugs—just the thought of it repulsed me. Psychotropics were like the worst kind of blasphemy, severing humanity's reliance on God's infinite healing power. I spent the next few months unemployed, sleeping excessively, chain-smoking, binge eating fast food, and leaving the house only to go to twelve-step meetings and therapy appointments.

Something had to give. I didn't want to work, and after my dramatic departure from Insight Intensive, I questioned whether or not I could find work, let alone get a positive referral. After a few weeks, I began researching graduate-school programs, thinking that a return to college might remedy my situation. I wanted to be more of an expert. I really did believe mental-health treatment options could be greatly improved by incorporating alternative therapies. I figured another degree could help me do that. Hopefully, by the time school started, my energy levels would have normalized. At least, that was the idea.

I wanted out of the clinical psychology field. I felt like my bipolar diagnosis was partially accurate but generally bogus, that the diagnosis itself was just a recent Western medical explanation for a timeless spiritual experience. I applied to return to Life University to pursue a doctor of chiropractic degree, in the hopes that I could better understand the psycho-neuroimmunological implications of my situation. Chiropractic training would allow me to learn more about the nervous system and alternative health options. If I was going to be able to address the science of spiritual emergence, I thought, I had better learn some science. Taylor and I deliberated, ultimately deciding the move to Atlanta was in our best interest. Both of us were embarrassed and ashamed of what had happened to me, and I think the move represented an escape, a fresh start.

Some couples' counseling and personal therapy around my hospitalization renewed our trust in each other, and amid some return to normalcy and the planning of our move, Taylor and I got pregnant with our first child. We had always talked about getting pregnant shortly after marriage, and even though we were on an obvious detour, we had faith that everything would work out. We were committed to each other, and we both wanted kids, so we figured, at the very least, nine months would be enough time to iron out the details and allow my full return to health.

Fatherhood represented an extraordinary impetus for change. Not only did I need to get healthy for the sake of my marriage, but I was about to be responsible for another life. Instead of rising to the challenge, though, I only fell further into my illness. The pressure was insurmountable. I could hardly fathom providing for myself, let alone a family. I started questioning if I should even be a father at all. I wondered how much of my condition was genetic. I questioned whether I would be able to prevent children from going down the same painful path of addiction and disorder. To think of putting a child through what I'd been through, of going through the heartache my parents had endured—it was terrifying.

When we moved to Atlanta, it became nearly impossible for me to continue denying my bipolar disorder. I had gained about forty pounds since being released from the hospital, most of which I attributed to depression. The demands of graduate school had me constantly on edge, and there were times I was so manic that I would leave class to draw graphs in the library, charting everything from reincarnation's role in embryological cell proliferation to the covalent bonds of God's love for humanity. Taylor lived in constant fear for my sanity and stability. As if that weren't enough, new parenthood presented levels of stress I'd never known existed.

That year, 2012, was the year of mixed moods, and I was hedging my bets, half expecting the Mayan prophecies to be correct. Despite growing concerns about my mood regulation and stress management, I continued my search for natural remedies to my suffering. I took supplements. I researched the mood implications of certain diets. I saw one of Atlanta's top chiropractors on a weekly basis. I meditated. I prayed. I did everything I could possibly think of to avoid pharmaceutical intervention. I suspected that if I just ate a sugar-free, dairy-free, grain-free, legume-free, caffeine-free, strict "paleo" diet; exercised for an hour every day; slept at least eight hours; meditated at least thirty minutes; let go of all my thoughts; worked minimally; and eliminated all relationship toxicity, I would never go crazy again.

After a few terms in school, I started realizing that chiropractic college wasn't for me. I had a one-track mind for spirituality and psychology, and the psychology of spirituality, and the spirituality of psychology. I began blogging and theorizing about enlightenment, even in the middle of my classes. I could barely concentrate on any of my assignments. I started working on an integrated model for enlightened living. I showed my family, hoping they would find it worth pursuing. I needed to write a book about it. The Dalai Lama could write my foreword. Eckhart Tolle could write my afterword. Deepak Chopra would colead my workshops. Oprah would promote my book. If I played all my cards right, when I turned thirty-five, I could run for president, with Marianne Williamson as my vice president, and we'd spearhead an enlightened society. This was the secret of manifesting abundance.

These moments of inspiration were all-consuming, though fleeting, and they would inevitably give way to the agony of real life. When I would put my son to bed at the end of a long day, when Taylor was both working full-time and caring for our child while I pretended to study and instead drew maps to God-consciousness, the piercing thought that I was sick would enter my mind. There were times I would sing to our baby, rocking him to sleep, and tears would start streaming down my face. In my heart, I knew there was no way I could be there for my family and continue surfing such enormous waves of madness. I needed to either leave or take medication. It was my choice to make.

Finally, Taylor wrote me a letter, sharing with me her plan to go back to Colorado with our son to live with her parents until I got help. She told me she loved me, but that she couldn't go on anymore. She was scared of the day that our child would be able to understand our fights, or worse, see me delusional.

Her concerns validated my greatest fears, but the thought of her leaving, the thought that I wasn't fit to raise my son, provided the necessary shock to my tired system. I could no longer live a life of denial. I could see the truth. I needed help. I begged her to stay, and I promised to finally get treatment, for good.

The pain of Taylor's intervention brought me to my knees. Praying to God felt like praying to myself, but I did it anyway. I was completely ready to surrender. I could no longer treat myself in pieces without healing the whole. All the parts of me, they were one. Maybe I could have kept it up, gone into hermitage, left my family, departed from this world, but I was too in love. I had always been in love.

I looked up a counselor who worked with the comorbidity of eating disorders, bipolar disorder, and addiction, and she referred me to a psychiatrist for the medical management of my mood. The shaky release of control felt right in my soul, though I still wondered what this life was really all about, and how far away was the God that dwelt in my heart.

As I accepted treatment and started taking medication, it was at first painfully difficult to pinpoint my true personality. How much of me was in there—had been there all along—and how much was the product of my condition? Was I an eccentric extrovert or a contemplative introvert? Was I really passionate about spiritual matters, or was I merely trying to justify my denial? Had God actually made me over, or was I delusional even in times of healing?

With the help of clinicians, I finally accepted that mental illness was more than the result of my life experience. Those events triggered and exacerbated some genetic predisposition that might or might not have expressed itself regardless. This was possibly why I was so drawn to God in my moments of sickness. I could see that the sum of my suffering was so much greater than those parts of my story. I hadn't been able to make sense of such strange thoughts and emotions.

In my continued search for spiritual significance, I saw that God didn't need me; I needed God. My backward relationship with the divine had caused so much religious and spiritual confusion. Grace required no compensation. God's gifts were free, untethered, waiting to be accepted. Salvation had always been available. I needed to forgive myself.

Over time, I came to believe that some parts of life are destined to remain a mystery. The magic I had been searching for lived in the vast stillness. In this ineffable space beyond my mind, the questions became the answers. I could feel an unshakable intuition that God had always been waiting, forever calling me to come home.

Epilogue

GO IN LOVE

I'm happy to share that this story ends in a place of overall sanity and productivity. To say that life is close to perfect would do a massive disservice, both to myself and to anyone else living a life of recovery from mental illness. I still struggle, not unlike any other person fearless enough to be honest. The difference today is that I don't fight it so hard. I have learned to savor the moments in which my heart is wide open, and I feel full of connection to the preciousness of life.

I hope that my journey offers some insight into the experience of mental illness. Just as cancer survivors stay aware that their cancer is in remission, recovery from mental illness includes the possibility of relapse. Just for today, life is beautiful. Maybe tomorrow, I'll look in the mirror and won't like what I see. Maybe next week, I'll feel depressed. Maybe next month, I'll need to take a new medication. Whatever lies ahead, I know I'll be able to handle it if I stay completely honest. The journey of life is a continual unfolding, and unlike the movies or even this book, it doesn't ever end. There is no happily ever after, just the momentary death and rebirth of the eternal now.

It's important to let you know that my recovery depends a great deal on the people around me. First and foremost, my wife is the biggest support I have, and there is no way I'd be where I am today without her unyielding love. Even with our love for each other, without proper education on *how* to express that love, our relationship would not be as solid as it is today. Humility is key. Anything in life worth having requires work and sacrifice, and marriage is no exception. I'm grateful to report that even a marriage with mental illness can be a fruitful one, and, as with most marriages, there are both great challenges and rich rewards.

Right behind my wife, and certainly throughout my entire life, is the love and support of my parents. They have never lost sight of what I like to think of as my soul-identity. When every aspect of my personality changed, when I had no idea who I was or what I was living for, my parents saw through the suffering, disorder, and behavior and held up the mirror of wisdom and clarity, refusing to let me lose sight of my true nature. Just as my wife and I have to work on how to best express our love for each other, parents and children need to do the same. The relationship between parent and child can be difficult enough without mental illness. We've had to be open and honest, apologize and forgive.

The reason I felt it was so important to tell my story was that I hoped to inspire others to face their own challenges. The hardest part of recovery was acceptance, and that acceptance was directly related to whether or not I believed health was possible. Today, I can promise: recovery is possible, but perfection is an illusion. Even though I live a life of general stability, I am never far from professionals trained to assist me in survival through the intricate nuances of recovery from mental illness. I spent over a decade in denial, and my sincerest prayer is that no person or their loved ones endure such needless suffering. Help is available, and recovery is real.

It's also critical that I address my arduous journey to accepting medication, since this is a very common challenge. There is little doubt in my mind that my bipolar disorder could be cared for without pharmaceutical intervention, but the extent to which every aspect of my life needs to be arranged in order to make it work is lunacy in itself. My unmedicated mind relentlessly calls for total abandonment of reality in the pursuit of a God made in my image. To try to control these impulses without medication is a painful burden, one that can only be managed in the strictest manner, and even then, the constant folly and subsequent shame sometimes grow so strong as to convince me that I'm the Antichrist. Any God that asks this of me is no God at all. To maintain loving relationships, to grow old with my wife, to father my children, to use my experiences in the service of others—this is a sacred life.

My delusions had me imagine that God would want me all to Himself, so I could teach His word, enlighten society, and save the world. This dangerous mixture of ego, fear, and ignorance is merely the result of narcissism combined with neurological overdrive. No one person is meant to play God. The word of God is alive in every human being. It's love. Love is the highest actualization of God and nature alike. Love is the common denominator, the intersection of faith and science. Love is where atheists, agnostics, and the followers of all religions rejoice. Love is inescapable, the driving force in each of us, whether in presence or in absence. I spent many years toiling over the complexities of spirituality, and I've returned to this most basic truth I learned as a child. Love was, and still is, the barometer by which we measure the worth of our lives.

As far as my spiritual practice is concerned, I have made peace with the realization that the part of me so desperately desiring to be enlightened is incompatible with the part of me that already is. The only guarantee is that I won't be around to witness my own enlightenment. My ego endlessly grasps for greater ground in the constant pursuit to use any and all spiritual experience as a way to feel superior. As the saying goes, "If you see Buddha on the path, slay Him." It's not until I transmute ego, by relaxing my mind and releasing thoughts, that wisdom shines through the gaps of neurosis. How can I live in congruence with my soul? How can I align myself with God's love? These are today's relevant questions, to which I only sometimes find the answers.

When it comes to God, we each call to mind our own conditioned conceptions. To use a common analogy, let's not throw the baby out with the bathwater. To me, God is like the baby whereas mental illness, ignorance, and confusion are the bathwater. I can say for sure that my beliefs about God have both hindered and assisted my recovery. There were times when God felt like the only power that could bring me to health, and there were also times when God became the only force in my way. Any sane person would call God into question under these circumstances. As someone with a history of psychosis, I have to guard myself against dogmatic and superstitious beliefs, or else I may have no relationship with God at all.

Jesus Christ Himself, in His last days, commanded, "'Love the Lord your God with all your heart and with all your soul and with all your mind.' This is the first and greatest commandment. And the second is like it: 'Love your neighbor as yourself.' All the Law and the Prophets hang on these two commandments."

Saint Teresa of Ávila, in her mystical classic *The Interior Castle*, elaborated, "Although we might have some clear indications that we are loving God, we can't be sure that we really are, but it is obvious whether or not we are loving each other. Be assured that the more progress you make in loving your neighbor, the greater will be your love for God."

I now know, where there is God, I am sure to find love, and where there is no love, I will discover only the myriad forms of ignorance. In any situation, I can ask myself, is this love, or is this delusion? In the end, there was only ever Love.

About the Author

Chris Cole holds a Bachelor of Arts in Contemplative Psychology from Naropa University and is a certified Strategic Intervention Coach. He works as a professional life coach, helping clients gain clarity and encouraging practical action toward a more purposeful existence. He wholeheartedly believes in the innate wisdom of people—their ability to choose health when given proper support. He resides in Atlanta, Georgia.

Connect with Chris and his work at thebodyofchris.com.

LIST OF PATRONS

This book was made possible in part by the following grand patrons who preordered the book on Inkshares.com. Thank you.

Adam Gomolin
Alice P. Weinstein
Allison C. Perkins
Austin Appleton
Barbara K. Laur
Bettie Sands
Cammy Hebert
C. Deming Fish
Darlene Whitmire
D. M. Hunt
Ellen Sullivan
Emma Mann-Meginniss
Gene Kansas
Harvey P. Cole
H. P. Chip Cole III
James H. Jackson
Jeffrey A. Hamm
Jeffrey Malucci
Jeffrey M. Forbes
Jessica Marano
Joan Hebert
Katherine D. Anderson
Kathy C. Appleton

Laura Rue
Lisa R. Drake
Mary B. Bignault
Mary Leigh E. Rogers
Maura E. Hagan
Michael A. Ferguson
P. A. Hagan
Pamela Klingbeil
Robert A. Takiguchi
Ryan Sullivan
Sheron L. Costas
Susan Sands
Susan S. Cole
Susan W. Ellington
Taylor H. Cleveland
Teresa Hebert
Tyler J. Cole
Tyler Perkins
Vann Cleveland

INKSHARES

Inkshares is a crowdfunded book publisher. We democratize publishing by having readers select the books we publish—we edit, design, print, distribute, and market any book that meets a pre-order threshold.

Interested in making a book idea come to life? Visit inkshares.com to find new book projects or to start your own.